Practical Pre-School

Healthy eating

Contents

Published by Step Forward Publishing Limited

St Jude's Church, Dulwich Road, Herne Hill, London SE24 0PB   Tel: 020 7738 5454

www.practicalpreschool.com   © Step Forward Publishing Limited 2007

Based on material published previously in Practical Pre-School and Practical Professional Child Care.
Healthy Eating ISBN-10: 1-904575-24-2 ISBN-13: 978-1-904575-24-5

Help yourself to water.

Introduction

Good nutrition is important for everyone. However, healthy eating is especially important for children as they are growing rapidly. They need all the energy and nutrients they can get.

Poor nutrition can impede children's ability to learn and achieve and also increases their risk of ill health.

One of the best things you can do is to be a good role model and let them watch and learn about healthy living by your own example.

The pre-school years are the ideal time to influence children's eating habits. If you provide meals or even just snacks, can you be sure that your influence is a good one?

Eating patterns in childhood often continue into adult life. Whether you offer meals or just snacks you have the chance to affect the long-term health of children in your care.

Eating is also a social and educational occasion and should be enjoyable. You can show this through the meals, snacks and drinks you provide as well as through what you teach and by example.

Food tasting and cooking sessions are popular and can be used to introduce children to new tastes and experiences. A wide range of books and resources are available on food – contact your local library or health promotion department for advice.

It helps if you let parents know your policies on food and drink, both at meal times and during sessions. Some settings include a statement about this in their prospectus. If children bring their own lunches you can help parents with ideas about what they can give their children.

You have two roles:

■ Teaching about food/healthy eating

■ If you provide food, making sure it is healthy.

Activities

You need to think about what you do in the wide context of Every Child Matters and helping children to 'be healthy'. Activities need to link to either

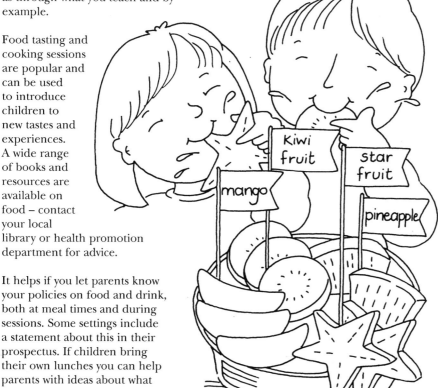

Birth to Three Matters or the Early Learning Goals, and also need to meet national standards. If you provide food, you need to make sure that you meet nutritional guidelines.

This book can help you with all of this.

The best approach is an integrated one – you need to be aware of healthy eating and healthy living in all that you do – from planned activities to everyday routines, so that you are giving consistent messages. Many settings do a topic on 'healthy eating' but this has no value if you forget about it once it has been done.

Drip feed

Involve children's families and the local community and take account of children's views and needs. Get together as a staff team to talk about the issues, look at your policies and ensure that you are taking a consistent approach.

The starting point must be what children already know – so make sure that you ask them and work from that.

As well as healthy eating, this is also about skills – helping the children to be self-confident, independent and able to make healthy choices for themselves.

Every child matters: being healthy

As well as meeting the National Standards you now need to help children to achieve the outcomes set out in the Children Act 2004. Liz Wilcock explains what each outcome means and suggests how you can adapt your practice to help children meet them. She starts with 'Being healthy'

The 14 National Standards are now grouped under five outcome headings. 'Being healthy' covers National Standards 7 (Health) and 8 (Food and drink). You need to consider the following:

- What does this outcome mean and what do you need to do?

- What will the inspector want to see?

Standard 7 – Health

It is expected that the registered person will promote good health, take positive steps to prevent the spread of infection and take appropriate measures when children are ill.

Hygiene

Hygiene must be a priority. Beyond personal hygiene, you are responsible for ensuring that children are cared for in clean surroundings. Ofsted will need to be kept informed of any significant health matters that a qualified medical person considers notifiable.

Staff should maintain good hygiene practices. Personal hygiene for staff as well as children needs consideration:

- Washing hands after using the toilet, and before handling any food.

- Encouraging children to blow their noses and dispose of the tissue in a lidded bin.

- All staff should be aware of procedures to deal with bodily fluids, and their disposal.

A rota system will ensure that all necessary cleaning and checking is carried out. Whilst it is important for your setting/home to be kept clean, the cleaning should not interfere with the time that children are being cared for.

- Do you have notices around your setting to remind adults to wash their hands?

- Do you keep nailbrushes and clean towels near washbasins?

- Are staff familiar with your health and safety policies and procedures? More importantly, do they follow the procedures? It is the responsibility of the registered person to ensure that staff are aware of all procedures, and adhere to them. A poster showing common illnesses can be placed on the noticeboard, with any other health/ hygiene information.

Environmental health officers will expect a good standard of hygiene. They can be contacted for advice if you have any queries about environmental health.

Giving medicine

Administering medicine to children takes organising. Who should be responsible? A room senior, deputy or manager should be overall responsible for all medications - never allow an unqualified person, or student, to give medication to a child.

Dosages, and the child's details, must be recorded, with a parent's signature written on the day, agreeing to you giving their child the prescribed medication. Consider the following:

- When liquid medicine is given to a child, do you pour from the opposite side of the bottle to the instructions? That way, if any liquid spills down the side of the bottle, the wording on the instructions will not be smeared.

- Do you check the medicine has not passed the 'use by' date?

- What procedures are in place for children to be given their medication on outings?

- Are parents in agreement that you will only give prescribed medication? The only time you may administer another medication is for a teething baby. Parents sometimes ask carers to give their baby Calpol, or similar, for 'when you need it'. You must not give Calpol to a baby or young child in your care, without the

parent giving you written agreement first. Your medication consent form should be worded to allow for this. Usually, if a baby is unwell, and you are concerned about teething, you may have to contact the parents – the baby may have a high temperature and need to be taken home. Think about the baby's needs first.

First aid

There should always be a first aider on site. A current certificate must be available for them – the certificate is current for a maximum of three years.

Sick children

You should consider that a sick child will be unsettled and perhaps frightened. One person should care for the child until either their parent or an ambulance arrives. The child will need plenty of love and reassurance.

You should have clear policies and procedures about how to deal with a

---

Birth to Three Matters

The four aspect headings within the Birth to Three framework are:

- A strong child

- A skilful communicator

- A competent learner

- A healthy child

How can you consider the aspect 'A healthy child' linked to the 'Being healthy' outcome?

- You need to develop close and warm relationships with the children in your care.

- You need to provide nutritious food and drink.

- You need to offer exciting experiences to allow children to cope with new situations in a safe, secure environment.

This will ensure that the youngest children in your care will be physically well, be energetic, begin to express their feelings and make healthy choices.

sick child. The documents should show the system you have in place to contact parents. Are your contact details up to date? Do you have emergency contact numbers? Check regularly with parents that contact numbers are correct. Do you have a sick room or quiet area for a sick child? This is important if the child has an infectious illness that you are trying to contain.

Good practice
Encourage children to understand about good health by:

- Spending time with children on topics related to health – teeth, food, exercise.

- Overcoming fears of going to the doctor /dentist /hospital.

- Using the home corner/role play to promote healthy living.

- Letting children tidy up and 'clean' – they enjoy this, when they are young!

- Making good use of any newsletters you send out to advise parents on current health issues, such as:

1. Infectious diseases

2. Head lice, conjunctivitis – and similar issues, when a child is not ill, but should be at home until treatment has been given.

3. How parents can get involved. Do any of your parents work in a health environment? Perhaps you can enlist their help.

- Invite health professionals to be involved with children directly.

Inspectors will want to see your written accident records (with parent signatures), medication and emergency record forms, your first aid box, and will want to discuss your arrangements for dealing with sick children.

Standard 8 – Food and drink

The registered person needs to make sure that children are provided with regular drinks and food in adequate quantities for their needs. Food and drink should be properly prepared, nutritious and comply with dietary and religious requirements.

Meals
You may provide up to three meals a day, with mid morning and mid afternoon snacks as well. As young children grow, they need a well balanced diet. Remember that children need to eat regularly.

There are four main groups of food to consider when you are meeting a child's dietary needs. These are:

Bread, cereals and potatoes
Fruit and vegetables
Milk and dairy foods
Meat and fish

Remember the vegetarian alternatives, such as pulses and soya. If a parent tells you that their child is vegetarian (not eating meat or fish) or vegan (not eating foods of animal origin – meat,

fish and diary produce), it will be a challenge to ensure that the child still has a balanced and nutritious diet to enable healthy development.

Good practice
- Whenever possible, try to keep to the child's own routine for meals.

- Babies who are bottle fed should be held and have warm physical contact during feed times.

- Parents should be advised daily if their child has not eaten the meals provided that day and told of any amounts left.

- Allow time for children to eat – let children eat slowly, as this is better for the digestive system.

- Make mealtimes a social time. If possible, staff should eat and drink with children to set a good example. If staff have separate meal breaks, they should still sit with children at the table and talk to them.

- Encourage good table manners.

- Children should go to the toilet and wash their hands before sitting to the table.

- Never leave children alone while they eat in case they choke.

- Store food correctly. Do not leave perishable food at room temperature for more than two hours.

- Your home corner could become the local fruit and vegetable shop. Some settings invite people in to cook with children, and talk about healthy ways to cook.

- The inspector will note from your booking/admission forms that children's dietary needs have been recorded. Your menus will show what meals are provided over a period of time, and should indicate a well balanced diet for all children.

- It is important that you regularly discuss children's changing dietary needs with parents.

Liz Wilcock, under-threes development officer, West Berkshire.

Standard 8 Food and drink Group care

The standard to be reached
Children are provided with regular drinks and food in adequate quantities for their needs. Food and drink is properly prepared, nutritious and complies with dietary and religious requirements.

What does this mean for your setting?

Promoting healthy eating patterns is difficult today, when so many children are in day care settings. Children may have meals or snacks at home, nursery, pre-school or out-of-school club. It may be that a packed lunch is provided for the children by the parents, or breakfast, lunch and tea is provided by the setting. Staff must recognise that children have different dietary or cultural needs. Menus should reflect this.

What do you need to do?

There are two main areas under this standard that need to be addressed. You need to consider criteria points 8.1 – 8.4.

Drinking water

It may seem obvious to say that children should be offered water throughout the day/session. However, it is surprising how many settings do not have water available to the children for when they ask for it, or just have it ready in jugs or bottles. Do the children know that they can have a drink whenever they want one? Thirst is not a comfortable feeling. Why should water, in particular, be offered? Water will quench a child's thirst and will not damage teeth. Some drinks are filling, and may affect a child's appetite. This does not mean that children should never be offered other drinks, but water offers the healthy choice as a drink to quench thirst – encourage children to help themselves if possible. Tap water is suitable for children. Many people now buy bottled water, but it has a higher level of salts, and may therefore not be suitable for young children. Other points to remember in respect of water are:

■ Temperature

Children will need more refreshments on a hot day – keep water cool and offer it regularly to the children.

■ Illness

A child may need to drink more if they are unwell.

Remember – recognise each child as an individual, and meet the child's needs.

Meals

You should offer interesting, nutritious meals to the children in your care. This is easier said than done if you are to meet individual needs. How can you do this?

Think about the meals you are able to provide. Whatever setting you work in, at some time during the day you will need to offer a snack, a main meal, more than one meal, treats, or you may be overseeing the children eat a packed lunch prepared by the parents. Consider the situation where you are providing three meals a day, in other words, offering full day care. You are responsible for ensuring that all dietary needs are met for the children each day – this will have an important effect on the child's health, and how eating habits will be formed.

Food should be nutritious. What do we mean by a nutritious diet for young children? In *A Practical Guide to Child Nutrition* by Angela Dare and Margaret O'Donovan (Stanley Thornes, ISBN 0 7487 2375 7) the authors state: 'Nutrients are the building blocks' of food which carry out the following functions:

■ providing warmth and energy to maintain body temperature and keep all organs and muscles working properly;

■ providing new material for growth;

■ maintaining and renewing body tissues;

■ keeping all the body processes, including the prevention of infection, in good order.

There are seven essential nutrients: proteins, carbohydrates, fats, vitamins, minerals, fibre and water. They each have a part to play in the growth and health of the body.

What is a varied diet? There are four main groups of food that need to be considered when you are meeting a child's dietary needs. These are:

Bread, cereals and potatoes
Fruit and vegetables
Milk and dairy foods
Meat and fish

Remember, too, the vegetarian alternatives, such as pulses and soya. If a parent tells you that their child is vegetarian (not eating meat or fish), or vegan (not eating foods of animal origin (meat, fish and dairy produce), you will have a challenge to ensure that the child still has a balanced and nutritious diet to enable healthy development. You will need to be guided by the parents on what the child may and may not eat. When menus are planned, use the information given to you by the parents. or, if possible, involve the children in making choices for the menu. It may be that the children have been involved in a cooking activity to provide the food for the snack or tea. Do you allow the children to be involved at mealtimes in the following ways?

■ Laying the table.

■ Counting how many children will need chairs/highchairs.

■ Older children acting as monitors, taking the snack around the table, offering to each child, and expecting a word of thanks.

Staff involvement

Do the staff consider the mealtime or snack time to be a social time with the children?

Do staff sit with children at tables and talk to them, or do they stand to one side with a cup of coffee making their own conversation? As a parent, which would you prefer to see?

Are meals served at the table, with staff asking children how much they would like to eat? Are second helpings offered?

Are the tables laid attractively? Some settings have tablecloths, and small vases of fresh flowers in the centre, manageable jugs of water for the children to help themselves and table placemats that the children have made for themselves for their own place.

Do staff feed the children, or encourage independent use of appropriate cutlery?

Parents
Clearly, the dietary information you need about each child will come from the parents. You need to respect children's feelings about likes and dislikes of certain foods, but also recognise that they may feel different if the meal they are offered is not the same as the other children's. How can you overcome this? Could you offer all the children a vegetarian meal, for example, once a week? Have you considered cultural differences? To include a varied and interesting diet to reflect other cultures is good for all the children.

In *Eating Well for the Under Fives in Childcare* (Caroline Walker Trust, ISBN 1 897820 07 0) there is useful information to help you in recognising food to celebrate festivals throughout the year.

There are several good books available about cooking for children in general. Your local bookseller will have a range to choose from – look specifically for those that consider meal planning, such as *The Baby and Toddler Meal Planner* by Anna Carmel (Ebury Press, ISBN 0 09 186360 0). The meals may be targeted at younger children, but they will give you inspiration for the older children, too!

How do all the staff know about each child's dietary needs? The parents will have advised the manager/supervisor of the setting of any specific needs when the child starts with you. The person preparing the meals should have a list of children in the kitchen area, showing special dietary or cultural requirements. The child's key worker, or staff responsible for the children in the room, should also be made aware of each child's dietary needs, and discuss this openly with the parents. Staff are not expected to have a full understanding of all dietary matters – this is very much a part of working with parents, and asking for information from them. The best policy is to be honest – if you don't know, say so! Parents will be happy to advise you on the best diet for their

SHAP calendar of religious festivals
SHAP Working Party
c/o National Society RE Centre
Church House
Great Smith Street
London SW1P 3NZ
Tel: 020 7898 1494

child – learn from this, and even ask for recipes that you could use. This would be an excellent example of good practice in working with the parents, and you would also be ensuring that you meet the child's dietary needs.

If parents provide lunchboxes for their children, you need to be careful. It may be that the child can only eat specific foods. Children need observing, as they will tend to help themselves to others food, particularly if it seems better than theirs! A member of staff should always be seated at the table to ensure that children with food from home eat only that food. Be advised by the environmental health officer on the storage of lunchboxes, particularly for holiday playschemes, if no fridges or cold store room is available. You may need to ask parents to place ice packs in the lunchboxes to keep the food cold.

Good practice
■ Children need to eat regularly.

Dealing with dilemmas

You are working in a nursery in the room where children aged three to five years are cared for. One male child, who has been with you for a short time, has a weight problem. Today, you overheard another child call him 'fatty'. The boy became upset and started crying. What can you do about this situation?

There may be a medical reason why the child is overweight. Children can be cruel at times, and not realise that they have hurt someone's feelings by calling them names. This particular issue can be dealt with as a larger group, when you talk to the children about 'How we feel when...'. This will enable all children to understand that everyone has feelings, and we should all try to make everyone feel good about themselves.

Staff should act as positive role models, by offering praise to the children for all their efforts and building self-esteem. A child with a medical condition that results in them becoming overweight needs much support from staff. Children need to be aware that we all have differences, and will have different strengths, too. Staff should promote each child's strengths in the setting.

A child who is overweight because of poor eating habits can be helped in other ways. It may be that the family would welcome some guidance in this area. How could you deal with this issue, without focusing on one family? The answer lies in your planning for topics. You can call the topic 'Ourselves' and plan to cover a number of issues that affect everyone, such as:

How we grow
Food that helps us to grow
How we look after ourselves
Teeth
Hair

Your home corner could become the local fruit and vegetable shop, and you could invite a variety of professional people/parents to visit the setting to talk to the children about a number of issues relating to food. Some settings invite people in to do cooking with children, and talk to them about healthy ways to cook.

For some families, finances are stretched. Sadly, many cheaper foods, which provide energy, are the main diet, whereas foods necessary for children's development, such as fruit and vegetables, are more expensive. If you can think of ways in which to help parents on a budget to look at the healthier options, you will be helping the children, too. You can also provide more opportunities for children to get exercise through your planning for physical development. Children will join in if you make games fun, and allow all children to achieve at some stage.

■ Store food correctly. Do not leave perishable food at room temperatures for more than two hours.

Remember – the environmental health department is available for advice.

What will the inspector be looking for?

Children's records indicating their dietary needs – *booking forms and kitchen area*

Your arrangements for providing food and drink – *menus and written policies*

How you find out about and meet children's dietary needs – *verbal discussion*

The arrangements you make when parents provide food and drink for their child – verbal discussion, named lunchboxes, fridge or cold store available. Ice packs requested from parents. Staff sit with children at mealtimes.

Whenever it is possible, try to keep to a child's own routine for meals.

■ Babies who are bottle fed should be held and have warm physical contact with the adult during feed times.

■ Parents should be advised daily if the child has not eaten the meals provided that day – and advised of any amounts left.

■ Allow time for children to eat – children need to be encouraged to eat slowly, as this is better for the digestive system.

■ Make mealtimes a social time. If possible, staff should eat and drink with the children, to set a good example. If staff have separate meal breaks, they should still sit with the children at the table, and talk to them.

■ Encourage good table manners.

■ Children should go to the toilet and wash their hands before sitting to the table.

■ Children under five years should not be left alone whilst they eat, in case they choke.

Standard 8 Food and drink Childminding

The standard to be reached
Children are provided with regular drinks and food in adequate quantities for their needs. Food and drink is properly prepared, nutritious and complies with dietary requirements.

You need to consider criteria points 8.1–8.3.

When you are shopping for food and drink, you need to consider not only the needs of your own children but the needs of the minded children, too. Some childminders keep a separate basket for the childminding food (for the purposes of having a receipt).

Should the food differ in any way to the food you are buying for your family? The answer is probably 'yes'. Your own family will have their likes and dislikes, and you will take this into account when you shop. Equally, your minded children may have specific dietary needs/preferences. You will have discussed this with the parents, and agreed on the food to be given to the child. This is likely to have been agreed in writing, in your contract with the parents.

An issue that usually arises is that of sweets and treats. You will, at some time, be taking the children out to the local shop, and the children may ask you for sweets. A good tip is to stick to one day of the week when you will treat the children - agree this with the parents first. Children will then come to understand that you only buy sweets on this one day. Be consistent in your approach – it does work!

Drinking water should be available to the children at all times. If possible, keep a jug of cool water ready to give to the children on request, or to help themselves as they get older. If you are out in the garden on a hot day, remember that the children will need refreshment, as well as yourself. Be prepared, take what you need outside with you, as you may not be able to go back indoors without taking all the

children with you, for example, if the paddling pool is out.

Think about healthy and nutritious snacks for the children – offer them food regularly. Allow children to help you prepare meals/snacks. Above all, regularly discuss the children's dietary needs with the parents. Children's needs change as they get older.

Birth to Three Matters: A healthy child

The 'Healthy child' aspect of *Birth to Three Matters* features four components:

■ Emotional well-being

■ Growing and developing

■ Keeping safe

■ Healthy choices

Although having nutritious food and being free from illness are important to children's overall physical health, this aspect acknowledges that young children need much more than that. Being cared for and special to someone is also vital to children's physical, social and emotional well-being.

Emotional well-being

This component focuses on young children needing close, warm and supportive relationships. They need to be able to express positive feelings such as joy, confidence and achievement, and negative feelings such as sadness, frustration and anger. This enables young children to recognise emotions and to develop strategies to cope with situations that are new, stressful or challenging.

Already social beings, 'Heads up, lookers and communicators' (aged 0-8 months) need to feel close attachments and special bonds with their carers. To build the loving relationships that babies crave, it's important that they have a key worker.

Key workers should interact with individual babies and regularly attend to their needs, both emotional and physical. Whenever possible, parents and key workers should hand their child directly over to one another at the beginning and end of sessions. This allows the child to move from the care of one person who is special to them to another, promoting feelings of emotional security.

'Sitters, standers and explorers' (aged 8-18 months) enjoy mutual, warm relationships with adults and other children. They may be affectionate and demonstrative, instigating cuddles for example, or coming to sit on a carer's lap.

Children increasingly express their feelings, which will be confusing and overwhelming at times. It's good practice for key workers and parents to liaise on how to respond to displays of strong emotion, such as anger. A consistent approach helps children to understand their feelings and learn how to cope with them.

Children may react badly to inevitable times in a group setting when their key worker is not present. It helps to prepare them by ensuring that they interact with other carers as well as their special person.

'Movers, shakers and players' (aged 18-24 months) have hopefully experienced several months of loving, responsive care, developing the confidence to move from a place of safety and security (the environment of their special adult) to explore the wider world in terms of environment, activities and people, happy in the knowledge they can return to their place of safety and security at any moment.

For instance, a child may leave their key worker to explore events across the room. After a few moments or minutes they may come back briefly, then set off again. The practitioner can support the child by acknowledging them and their adventure on their return visits – 'Hello! Have you been playing with the balls?'

'Walkers, pretenders and explorers' (aged 24-36 months) continue to grow in confidence. They will increasingly be able to do things independently, such as going to the toilet. However, children still need to know they can depend on carers to be close by.

The knowledge that a trusted adult is on hand to give help and support if needed, boosts children's confidence to attempt independence and try new things. You can help by encouraging and praising children's efforts, as well as their achievements.

Growing and developing

'Growing and developing' focuses on meeting children's physical needs, which is essential for health and well-being. This component acknowledges that children who are physically well will have the energy and enthusiasm to benefit from the activities available to them.

'Heads up, lookers and communicators' can thrive only when their nutritional, physical and emotional needs are met. At this stage it's important that key workers and parents liaise closely about feeding and sleeping details, so that the overall picture of a baby's daily routine is not lost. Practitioners can also encourage and help mothers who wish to continue breastfeeding their babies.

'Sitters, standers and explorers' will increasingly become more independent in feeding themselves. It's beneficial to make mealtimes an enjoyable, social occasion, which encourages children to enjoy both their food and the experience of sitting around the table, even if they're in a highchair.

Children are also likely to be settling into new sleeping routines. Regular rest is still important, but children will begin to sleep less in the daytime.

This component tells us that 'Movers, shakers and players' 'have a biological drive to use their bodies and develop their physical skills'. These children need plenty of opportunities and space to run and play. To enable children to practise and develop new physical skills, you must provide access to appropriate resources and equipment, such as low slides, balls and large interlocking bricks.

'Walkers, talkers and pretenders' are increasingly gaining control of their own bodies. Their large and fine motor skills are becoming more refined, and they are ready to tackle more sophisticated physical movements, such as turning the pages of a book and riding large wheeled toys. They will also be gaining control of their bladder and bowels. Encourage independence but offer support and help when it's needed.

Keeping safe

This component stresses that to keep safe and protected, young children need a developing sense of when and how to ask for adult help. It's closely linked to the component 'Healthy choices' (see below).

'Heads up, lookers and communicators' already make purposeful movements and this component points out that babies 'tend not to stay in the position in which they have been placed'. It's the responsibility of carers to ensure that children have an increasing choice in their environment, within safe and supervised limits.

'Sitters, standers and explorers' often have little awareness of danger. This is the time when young children are beginning to walk, run and climb, and so striking a balance between challenge, freedom and safe boundaries is paramount. It's important to be consistent and to acknowledge that children of this age are more focussed on what they want to do, than on their own safety.

This component reminds us that the need 'Movers, shakers and players' have for attention and affection, coupled with their increasing independence, makes them particularly vulnerable. All those involved in their care should be aware of

---

A strong child

The concept of 'A strong child' runs throughout the framework. Being a holistically healthy child will enable children to be strong - meaning capable, confident and self-assured.

---

how to promote safety, including good practice in the area of child protection.

Healthy choices

Children gradually learn to make healthy choices in regards to their own bodies and what they can and can't do. 'Healthy choices' is closely linked to 'Keeping safe'.

This component tells us that 'Heads up, lookers and communicators' 'show preferences for people and for what they want to see, hear and taste'. Practitioners can become responsive carers by taking note of, and acting upon, these preferences.

By the time they are 'Sitters, standers and explorers', children and their carers will be developing a clearer picture of their individual likes and dislikes. Simple choices and decisions will be made frequently and these can be supported by adults. Encourage considered behaviour by presenting options during this stage – 'Would you like water or juice today?'

The increasing exploration by 'Movers, shakers and players' may mean their choices involve risk. While taking risks shouldn't be inhibited, carers must ensure that children's safety is not compromised – this is something of a balancing act that becomes easier with experience and expertise.

'Walkers, talkers and pretenders' start to understand more clearly that the choices they make have consequences. They're beginning to consider the consequences of their behaviour before and during their actions. At this stage it's beneficial for practitioners and parents to use the same strategies consistently to promote positive behaviour, so that children develop a clear understanding of consequences and are not confused.

Miranda Walker is an early years and playwork trainer, writer and speaker. She owns her own day care settings in Devon.

Foundation Stage activities: links with learning

Keeping healthy through eating well and taking exercise is surely a central part of educating and nurturing young children. The need to eat healthily may be subject to social and political trends but it never goes away and as such practical activities designed to reinforce a healthy lifestyle are essential to our early year's curriculum. These activities also seem to span all the early learning goals and are positive opportunities for children to make links in their learning. Children will 'recognise the importance of keeping healthy and those things which contribute to this' (Physical development) as they share a healthy fruity breakfast together and at the same time they will 'interact with others and take turns in conversation' (Communication, language and literacy). As they celebrate Chinese new year and eat noodles with chopsticks they will learn to 'respect cultures and beliefs of others' (Personal, social and emotional development). As they count and sort the apples at the Apple Variety Show they will be 'counting reliably' (Mathematical development) and 'investigating objects and materials by using all of their senses as appropriate (Knowledge and Understanding of the World). The list goes on… The involvement of parents in partnership with practitioners is clearly required for all these ideas to be put into practice at home and in the setting for the benefit of the whole child.

Personal, social and emotional development

- Read *Oliver's Vegetables* by Vivian French. Share different vegetables, raw and cooked with the children. Who has a favourite vegetable? Which is the most popular vegetable in the class? Encourage them to try new tastes.

- Fill a large shallow tray with assorted dried pasta and some cooking implements such as saucepans, lids, spoons, sieves and bowls. Encourage the children to talk about the meals they are making and how they will make them more healthy.

- Share breakfast one morning with the children. Make this 'fruit breakfast mix' by layering the ingredients in clear bowls or glasses. Use chopped fresh or tinned pineapple, raspberries, chopped banana, chopped dates or raisins, vanilla yoghurt, bran flakes or cornflakes.

- Read *Pumpkin Soup* by Helen Cooper and talk about taking turns, sharing and friendship. What things do the children like to do with their friends. Work together to make some pumpkin or vegetable soup. Let everyone have a turn at stirring the soup.

- Make a selection of food from different countries. Involve parents and adult carers in contributing or cooking food, if possible. Try samosas, bhajis, rice, spring rolls, prawn crackers, noodles, French bread, pizza, tacos, banana bread, and so on. Share food with children and talk about the country, ingredients, who made it and why it's special. Which is the healthiest food? Which is their favourite new food?

- At circle time, play this singing game about favourite healthy foods.

I like tomatoes
Echo Adam likes tomatoes
I like tomatoes
Echo Adam likes tomatoes
They're red and juicy and
fun to eat
Echo They're red and juicy and
fun to eat
I like tomatoes
Echo Adam likes tomatoes
[Sing to the tune of 'Three blind mice']

- Go on a trip to the local supermarket or outdoor market and identify and name all the fruit and vegetables. Ask the children to pick out a new yellow or red fruit or vegetable in the produce aisle. Buy a selection of unusual fruit and organise a 'blind fruit tasting'. Use toothpicks to pick up and sample the different fruits. Can the children identify them when they are wearing a blindfold?

- Play the 'Good food fishing game'. Ask the children to cut out pictures of food from the five basic food groups and stick them onto fish shapes. Put a paper clip onto each fish. Using a fishing rod made from dowelling, string and a small magnet go fishing!. Label five pots with the name of each food group, 1 = cereals, 2 = fruit and veg. 3 = dairy products, 4 = protein, meat and fish, 5 = sugars and sweets, and ask the children to put their catch into the right pot.

Communication, language and literacy

- Open a 'health food shop' or café in the role-play area. Make, buy and sell healthy food in the café. Which healthy meals and snacks will they include on the menu? Try fruit juices, salads, cereal bars, homemade soups, fresh bread, etc. Invite the children to take on roles of waiter, chef, customer, farmer, etc.

- Write out healthy shopping lists to take to the health food shop. Also ask the children to write alternative unhealthy lists for fun. Do they understand the difference?

■ Read *The very hungry caterpillar* by Eric Carle. Rewrite the story calling it 'The very healthy caterpillar' and only include healthy food in the caterpillar's diet!

■ Make a list of describing words for healthy foods, such as spicy, tangy, raw, diet, tasty, sweet, salty, low-fat, etc. Use with healthy food such as fruit and vegetables and encourage alliteration, for instance 'great grapes', 'tasty tomatoes', and 'low fat leeks'. Combine the phrases into tongue twisters.

■ Make a healthy recipe book called 'Eat Well, Keep Well'. Ask the children to bring in ideas from home and extended family. Laminate

recipes for the children to choose to read and create in the home corner. Alternatively, make them into a book to sell to parents and raise funds.

■ Read *Eat your peas* by Kes Gray. Help the children to rewrite the story by choosing a different vegetable they don't like. Daisy's mum promises all sorts of treats such as '100 puddings, 10 new bikes and a chocolate factory'. What sort of bribes can the children make up? And what will their mum have to eat at the end?

■ Ask the children to keep a healthy food diary over the weekend. Provide them with a photocopied sheet of sentences to finish such as 'On Saturday, at breakfast/lunch/ dinner I ate...............' and 'I ate .... for a healthy snack'.

■ Try some fruity riddles. 'I'm thinking of something round......green...... juicy......[apple] or long......... green.........stringy......?

■ Take some obscure photographs of fruit and vegetables from funny angles and close up using a digital camera. Try zooming in on the florets of a cauliflower or a close-up cross section of a pineapple. Can the children identify the different healthy food. Put them on the wall and ask the parents to have a go too!

Mathematical development

■ Ask the children to work with a partner to make 'patterned fruit kebabs'. Let them choose 3 or 4 different fruits that they both like to eat from a selection. Can they make a repeating pattern as they thread the fruit onto a kebab stick?

■ Talk about the 'Five-a-day' fruit and vegetable scheme to the children and their parents. Help the children to try and eat 5 portions of fruit and vegetables every day.

■ Choose 4 or 5 different fruit and make a tally chart of the children's favourite fruit. Convert the information into a picture graph. Which is the least popular fruit?

■ Sing some healthy number rhymes such as '5 fat-free sausages frying in a pan', '5 wholemeal buns in a baker's shop', '5 fresh peas in a peapod pressed' and 10 green bottles of water'!

■ Buy an assortment of fresh vegetables for the children to look at and handle. Ask them to sort them according to colour, size, shape, texture and weight.

■ Ask the children to design a pure fruit smoothie using some of their favourite fruit. Here are two examples: 1 banana, 2 kiwi fruit, 5 strawberries or 1 banana, half a melon, 2 nectarines. Blend the fruit together and add some ice. Add apple juice to get the right consistency if necessary.

■ Make a card template of a lunch box shape and ask the children to draw round it onto a piece of paper. Can they draw or stick onto it an ideal healthy lunch of 2 cheese sandwiches, 5 carrot sticks, 1 apple, 10 raisins, 1 yoghurt, 2 drinks, etc.

■ Talk about mealtimes. Use clock faces to show the different times for breakfast, lunch and dinner. Ask the children to draw or write what their favourite healthy food is for each mealtime.

■ Organise an 'Apple variety show'. Choose about 6 different varieties of apple and ask the children to sort them according to colour, size, weight, taste, etc. Which is the smallest? Heaviest? Reddest? Use the different variety names such as 'Granny Smith', 'Golden delicious', or 'Braeburn'. Can the children guess where these names originate from? Which apple tastes the best?

■ Cut up an apple and look at the seeds. Count the seeds. Cut up another apple and do the same. Plant the seeds in compost and wait for them to grow.

■ Read *Handa's Surprise* by Eileen Browne. Use the pictures to practise counting backwards from 7 and subtraction skills as the fruit is consumed by the naughty animals. Help the children to act out the story using real or plastic fruit.

Knowledge and understanding of the world

■ Grow your own healthy food. Try cherry tomatoes or French beans in gro-bags in the outside area or garden. Place against the wall and use bamboo canes to provide the plants with support. Lettuce, radishes and herbs are also quite straightforward to grow. Plant seeds in a shallow dish of soil or compost with gravel in the base. Keep on a sunny windowsill and water regularly.

■ Grow a row of root-tops! Cut 2cm tops off a selection of root vegetables such as carrots, parsnips, beetroot and turnips and place them in shallow tray lined with pebbles. Fill with water to cover the base of each vegetable and wait for the hair to sprout!

■ Try growing bean sprouts for a healthy snack. Put whole dried pulses, beans, chickpeas or lentils in a tray and add water. You may need to change the water two or three times a day. The beans will quickly start

sprouting and after a few days can be eaten raw, stir fried, or in sandwiches to add extra crunch. They are a good source of vitamins and protein so once the first lot have been eaten, grow some more!

■ Talk about why we all need food. How do the children feel when they are hungry? (Tummy rumbles, grumpy mood, find it hard to concentrate.) How do they feel when they have eaten too much? (Full, sick, stuffed, etc.) Our bodies tell us when we need food and how much we

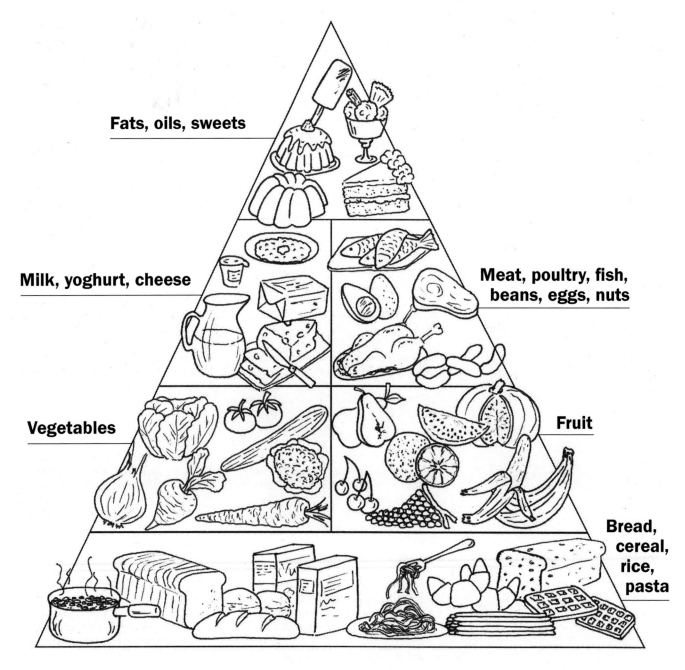

Fats, oils, sweets

Milk, yoghurt, cheese

Meat, poultry, fish, beans, eggs, nuts

Vegetables

Fruit

Bread, cereal, rice, pasta

need to eat. Ask the children to draw 2 pictures of themselves and label them: 'This is me when I'm hungry' and 'This is me when I have eaten some healthy food'.

■ Introduce the food pyramid (see left) and explain that the children need to eat a balanced diet from the five basic food groups in order to be healthy. The pyramid helps us to eat healthy food in the right proportions i.e. more from the bottom group than the top! Give the children a blank pyramid to fill in with cut out pictures of the different types of food.

■ All food comes from plants or animals. Use food cards or the actual food and play a game to see how many common foods children can identify as originating from a plant or animal? Have 2 big sorting hoops, a green one for plants, and a red one for animals. Which hoop will the cheese go in?

■ Sort vegetables into those that grow underground i.e. root vegetables and those that grow above the ground. Draw a picture to show where they grow.

■ Explore food from different cultures. Celebrate Chinese New Year and try eating noodles with chopsticks! Try some Indian delicacies during Diwali. Find out about different food related to festivals in this country. What do children like to eat at Halloween or on Bonfire night?

■ Take a 'Bread trip around the world' and taste pitta bread from Greece, naan bread from India, baguettes from France, breadsticks or tortillas from Italy, rye bread from Sweden, and bagels from the USA.

■ Use a bread machine to make fresh bread. Examine, measure and smell the ingredients. Talk about how the ingredients will combine into dough. Enjoy the smell of the bread as it cooks. Share the bread together for snack.

■ Trace the journey of some fruit and vegetables from other countries to our tables for instance 'lemons' from Italy or 'chillies' from South America.

Physical development

■ Talk about how food helps our bodies in three main ways: to grow, to be active, and to keep fit and healthy. Illustrate this with a game. Ask the children to move around the room taking care not to bump into each other as you shake a tambourine. When you tap the tambourine once they must stop and grow as tall as they can, stretching up to the sky. Two taps signals a different activity – such as running up and down on the spot or five star jumps. Finally, tap the tambourine three times and shout 'How are you today?' for the children to reply 'Fit and healthy thank you!'.

■ Make salt dough fruit and vegetables to sell in the role play health food shop.

■ Fill a shallow tray with a selection of dried pulses and seeds. Ask the children to sort the seeds into pots using only tweezers. How quickly can they find five beans?

■ Make a mixture of salt, rice and dried beans in a bowl and ask the children to separate them into three bowls using a sieve and a colander.

■ Organise a keep fit session to music for the children and their parents or carers. Talk about how exercise and a balanced diet work together to keep us healthy.

■ Play 'fruit salad'. Ask the children to stand in a circle and give each child the name of a fruit: apples, pears, bananas, oranges. Then ask all the oranges or all the apples to swap places. When you shout 'fruit salad' all the children have to swap places. Chaos!

■ Hold a 'crazy fruit and veg. olympics' with lots of games using fruit and vegetables. Try building and balancing with carrot sticks, bobbing for apples, eating grapes from a mountain of flour, passing oranges along the line under the chin, and

the 'chocolate game' using raw vegetables.

■ Let the children use tools to peel, chop and prepare vegetables to make soup or stir fry. Try onions, potatoes, leeks and carrots for a tasty soup or peppers, mushrooms, carrots and courgettes for stir fry.

■ Try raw and cooked versions of different fruit and vegetables such as carrots, apples, tomatoes, plums, etc. Do the children prefer to eat them cooked or raw?

■ Replace 'duck duck goose' game with new words, i.e. 'corn, corn, carrot' or 'grape, grape, apple'.

■ Create a healthy food fruit machine. Place three real or plastic apples, oranges and bananas in a box. Ask three children to stand behind the box and on your signal pull out one fruit each. If they show three of the same fruit, you win a prize – a piece of fruit! Add some sound effects such as a vibraslap or maraca as the fruit emerge.

Creative development

■ Use modroc wrapped round scrunched up newspaper to create fruit shapes. When dry paint the fruit and arrange in giant fruit bowls to

make 3D still life pictures.

- Create collages of healthy meals on paper plates. Contrast with unhealthy plates full of sweets! Use to make a wall display as a reminder for the children of what they should be eating.

- Make posters for the health food shop using pictures cut out of magazines or the children's own paintings.

- Try painting and printing with fresh fruit and vegetables. Slice them in different ways and put assorted colours of paint in shallow trays. Use the carrot tops and celery leaves as paint brushes.

- Sing this healthy food song to the tune of 'Little Brown Jug':

  Spinach, peas and broccoli
  I like food that's good for me.
  Apples, pears and strawberries,
  Can I have some for my tea?

  Try writing a second verse with different food included in lines 2 and 4.

- Try this new version of Old MacDonald.

  Old MacDonald had a farm
  EIEIO
  And on that farm he grew some veg.
  EIEIO
  With fresh peas here, fresh peas there
  Fresh peas, fresh peas everywhere…

- Retell the story of *The Enormous Turnip*. Invite the children to act out the roles of different characters as they all attempt to pull up the mighty vegetable. Have fun when the mouse succeeds where all the people failed!

- Use the names of fruit and vegetables to create Five a day healthy chants. Try 'Five a day, five a day, we must eat, five a day', and then add some new lines. Ask the children to work in pairs and choose two fruit or vegetables to organise into a rhythmic chant. Start with apples, grapes, apples, grapes or oranges, bananas, oranges, bananas. Ask them to say and clap the rhythm patterns of the words. Add instruments to keep the beat.

- Sing this song to the tune of 'Messing about on the river':

  Carrots and beans,
  Eat up your greens,
  Let's eat them all together.
  Apples and plums,
  Fill up your tums,
  Let's eat them all together.

- Provide the children with lots of different coloured paper, felt and materials and help them to cut out shapes. Stick onto circles of card and create super healthy pizzas.

- Let the children use scissors and paper to create giant mouths using red paper for lips and shiny white paper for teeth. Mount them on black sugar paper. Talk to the children about looking after their teeth so they stay white and shiny!

- Make observational drawings of cut and whole fruit and vegetables.

- Show the children some famous paintings of still life by artists such as Cezanne, Van Gogh and Juan Gris. Help them to make a display of fruit, vegetables and other suitable items and then have a go at painting a still life. Mount the pictures with frames and display as if in a gallery. Make a catalogue of the children's work so parents can visit and admire or even purchase the artwork!

Feeding pre-school children: guidelines and good practice

On 19 May 2006, the Secretary of State announced a suite of new nutritional standards for school lunches as well as food and drink served at other times of the day. The first set of standards, the food-based standards for lunch, came into force in September 2006. These apply to all local authority primary, secondary and special schools in England. Subsequent regulations will set out the final food and nutrient-based standards which will apply to food served at other times of the day.

The Interim Food-Based Standards for school lunches 2006 (Primary, secondary and special schools) can be found on www.teachernet.gov.uk/wholeschool/healthyliving

Unfortunately at present only the school lunch standards are statutory. The school meals review panel (SMRP) recommended that pre-school and young people in other settings should be similarly protected. The Early Years Foundation Stage (EYFS) framework places a specific welfare requirement on providers that "children are provided with nutritious food and drink to meet their needs". The EYFS will also include good practice for providers. Providers will be directed to a range of information about nutritional standards, including the updated Caroline Walker Trust guidance on which the new school meals standards are modelled.

The Food Standards Agency (FSA) provided a grant to the Caroline Walker Trust, to update its guidance "Eating Well for the under-5s in Child care". This also has an associated menu planner and training pack (including CD ROM) (see box).

The only standards that currently apply to nursery schools are those found in the document "Healthy school Lunches for pupils in nursery schools/units". This was published in 2000 and can be found on the DfES website. These standards became compulsory from 1 April 2001.

Although the legislation in these doesn't apply to private nurseries or childminders, they contain practical and useful guidance which can be used by anyone catering for the pre-school age group. Furthermore, it is likely that through the EYFS framework

more rigorous food standards and additional nutritional standards may be introduced. The 2001 standards provide an excellent stepping stone of good practice for all pre-school providers.

The document takes a practical and common sense approach. When asking, 'What is a healthy diet?' it states: 'There are no healthy or unhealthy foods, only healthy or unhealthy diets. For children aged five and under a healthy diet means broadly:

- A balanced diet with plenty of variety

- A diet which provides enough energy for satisfactory growth and development

- Plenty of fruit and vegetables

- Plenty of iron-rich foods

- Plenty of calcium-rich foods

- Not having sugary foods and drinks too often.

What are the compulsory standards?

The standards say that for lunches for children in nursery schools or units, at least one item from each of the following food groups must be available every day:

About Eating Well for under-5's in childcare – Caroline Walker Trust

This comprehensive report provides clear practical and nutritional guidelines for under 5's in child care. It covers a wide range of topics relating to food and health including:

- appropriate milks for babies and infants

- appropriate drinks for infants and under 5's

- physical activity

- food for children with special needs

- vegetarian and special diets

- dealing with food refusal

- diet and behaviour

- food related customs

The nutrient based standards are divided into different age groups and different meals and snacks within that, hence ensuring appropriate balance of food throughout the day. This ensures that children in full time child care and those visiting for only small periods of time have an appropriate proportion of their food requirements during that time.

The training Materials and CD ROM provide further practical help and guidance on interpreting the guidelines and looks at a number of issues, including:

- the factors influencing the choice of the food we and pre-schoolers eat

- the consequences of typical eating patterns

- how pre-schoolers become obese and what to do about it

- questionnaires to check your knowledge of nutritional issues for early years

- snack ideas

- reducing salt and sugar intakes

- dealing with allergy and other special diets

- encouraging eating well

- developing food policy

You can obtain a copy of the booklet, "Eating well for under-fives in child care", for £20.00 from The Caroline Walker Trust. The training materials are also priced £20.00 or if buying two together £30.00. The order form can be downloaded from the website www.cwt.org.uk or contact Caroline Walker Trust at 22 Kindersley Way, Abbots Langley, Hertfordshire WD5 0DQ. Telephone: 01923 269902

- Starchy foods such as bread, potatoes, rice and pasta;

- Fruit and vegetables;

- Milk and dairy foods;

- Meat, fish and other non-dairy sources of protein.

The document points out that these are minimum standards. Some local education authorities may have higher standards and those should continue.

There are also some additional recommendations. Although these are not in the regulations, the Secretary of State:

- Expects that drinking water should be available to all children every day, free of charge;

- Strongly recommends that schools should offer some hot food, particularly in the winter months. A school lunch does not have to be a hot meal. However, a hot meal can be a useful morale booster during the colder months. Parents often prefer to buy a hot meal for their children and see it as offering added value; and

- Strongly recommends that drinking milk is available as an option every day.

Good practice

The standards include a chapter on 'Good catering practice', which includes useful and practical advice on meeting the standards and planning menus.

Healthy School Lunches for Pupils in Nursery Schools/Units: Guidance for School Caterers on Implementing National Nutritional Standards is published by the DfES and available from:

DfES Publications
PO Box 5050
Sherwood Park
Annesley
Nottingham NG15 0DJ

Telephone: 0845 602 2260

The reference that you need to quote is: DfES 314/2000

The publication is also available on www.dfes.gov.uk/schoollunches

Good sources of iron which are well absorbed
- canned sardines, pilchards, mackerel, tuna, shrimps, crab

- liver pate and sausage, kidney, heart

- lean beef, lamb, pork: roast, mince, burgers, liver

- chicken or turkey, especially dark meat, liver

- sausages, grilled

- fish paste

For example, within the 'Bread, other cereals and potato' section it gives the following advice:

Points worth remembering when frying potatoes:

- Large pieces of potato, thick or straight cut chips, absorb less fat than thin or crinkle-cut chips

- Try to use a frying fat or oil which contains not more than 20 per cent saturated fat

- Have the oil at the correct temperature, change it regularly and drain it off well.

Similar practical advice is given within each food group. For example:

Meat and fish
Try to select the leanest cuts of meat you can afford and trim off any visible fat and take the skins off chicken. Drain or skim the fat from casseroles and mince wherever possible.

It is strongly recommended that servings of fish should include oily fish, such as sardines and mackerel which contain a type of fat beneficial to health.

Milk and dairy products
Milk and dairy products are an excellent source of calcium, which is important for good bone development. Skimmed milk is not suitable as a main drink for the under-fives. Whole or semi-skimmed milk should be used for this age group.

Do not rely too much on cheese as the main protein, for example for vegetarians. Try not to serve it more than once a week as the only vegetarian option.

Foods containing fat and sugar
Aim to keep the proportion of foods in this group to no more than about one tenth of the total food on offer over the course of a week. Try not to offer more than one fried item a day.

Use monounsaturated and polyunsaturated fats wherever possible for cooking, spreading and in dressings. Saturated fats include hard margarines, lard, suet and coconut oil. Monounsaturated and polyunsaturated fats include maize, corn, safflower, sunflower, Soya, rapeseed, olive oils and spreads made from these oils.

Ice cream can be high in fat. Try not to serve ice cream as a dessert too often. Try non-dairy ice cream as an alternative.

Fresh, tinned and dried fruit can be incorporated into puddings. Dried fruit provides extra fibre.

Fruit and vegetables
Fruit and vegetables can be fresh, frozen, dried, canned or in juice form. Dried fruit is a good source of iron.

Steaming or cooking vegetables with minimal amounts of water, and serving as soon after cooking as possible, helps to retain nutrients. Long cooking times and keeping vegetables warm for long periods before serving will lead to heavy loss of some nutrients.

It is good to see the following statement within the 'Vegetables' section: 'Spaghetti hoops and other canned pasta in tomato sauce should not be served as a vegetable, but counted as part of the starchy food group'. This change alone will result in an

Rich sources of folic acid
- fresh raw or cooked brussels sprouts, asparagus, spinach, cooked black eye beans

- breakfast cereals (fortified with folic acid)

- liver

Other good sources
- fresh, raw, frozen and cooked broccoli, spring greens, cabbage, green beans, cauliflower, peas, bean sprouts, okra, cooked soya beans, iceberg lettuce, parsnips, chick peas

- kidneys, yeast and beef extract

Good sources of zinc
- lean beef, lamb, pork: roast, mince, burgers, liver
- chicken or turkey, especially dark meat, liver
- sausages
- hard cheeses
- eggs
- tinned pilchards, sardines, and tuna
- brown and wholemeal bread
- whole grain breakfast cereals
- red kidney beans, chick peas, lentils, nuts

improved vitamin C and folic acid intake. This in turn may well result in an improved absorption of iron. It also teaches children that spaghetti is part of the starchy food group and not a vegetable.

The document also covers:

- Monitoring nutritional standards

- Improving the service – this section looks at pricing and promoting uptake of meals.

- Special dietary requirements – considers religious and ethnic groups, vegetarians and allergies.

I used the self-monitoring check-list to assess the lunch menu from a local day nursery. I found it a useful tool that quickly and easily gave an indication of the nutritional quality of the menu

Good sources of calcium
- hard cheeses, cheese spread, soya cheese
- canned sardines or salmon, drained and mashed up with the bones, fish paste
- tofu (soya bean) steamed or spread
- milk and yoghurt
- soya drink with added calcium
- soya mince
- ice cream
- egg yolk
- bread (except wholemeal), crumpets, muffins, plain and cheese scones
- beans, lentils, chick peas
- ready to eat or stewed figs

The Government recommends that school caterers keep records of the food provided:

- to check that they are meeting national nutritional standards every day

- to see what items are being eaten. For example, are some foods running out too early? Are some dishes always left over? What foods are not being eaten?

- as a record of whether they are implementing healthier catering practices

Reliable sources of information

So, who might you turn to if you are interested in taking an in-depth look at your menus or want some ideas for promoting a healthy diet? In the UK, state-registered dieticians and registered public health nutritionists are the professionals qualified to provide advice and training on good nutrition in public settings.

State-registered dietitians are qualified to translate the science of nutrition into practical advice. They can be found working in a variety of areas. About half are employed by the NHS. The remaining 50 per cent work in education, industry, research or as freelance consultants. Of those employed by the NHS a wide variety of roles are undertaken. Some specialise in clinical settings, working on children's wards or with patients with kidney or liver failure. Others work in the community, sometimes with GPs or promoting health

of the general population, with the aim of disease prevention.

Community or health promotion dieticians would generally be the ones who work with teachers and care staff and you may well have access to one locally. Some dieticians may have a specific remit to work with schools, others may have more difficulty finding time to advise you.

To discover what dietetic services are available in your area, you can contact your local hospital and ask to speak to the dietetic department. Ask them if there is a community or health promotion dietician.

Alternatively, you could employ your own dietitian for a project. To make contact with a freelance dietitian visit http://www.dietitiansunlimited.co.uk/

Local authority health promotion departments sometimes have an officer allocated specifically for under 5's and if they don't they will certainly have a resources officer. To contact your nearest health promotion department or service try looking in your local phone book. Alternatively, you can phone your local health authority or health trust, which should be able to give you the number.

Beverley Spicer, community paediatric dietician.

The importance of snack and mealtimes

Most pre-school groups sit down together and share food – whether it be a meal or a slice of apple. This may be a break from play but it's certainly not a break from learning. Chris Heald explains why it's so important to plan and prepare for this time as much as you would any other activity

Imagine that you are in a restaurant, but instead of tablecloths, the tables are bare. When you try to choose your seat, the waiter tells you to sit next to a stranger. There is no choice, you get what you are given and you must eat it.

When the food comes, it is piled in a bowl. When you ask for bread, one of the waiters picks up a piece from a central plate and throws it across the table for you. There is only a spoon to eat with. When you try to make conversation with the person sitting next to you, the waiter tells you to be quiet. When you can't eat all your food, because you don't like some of it, the waiter tells you that you can't go back to work until you've finished it.

Have you stepped onto the set of *Fawlty Towers*? No, you are just experiencing what some young children experience every day during their snack or mealtimes, simply because the adults in charge have not taken time to think about what it is like to be a child in their setting.

Eating out is a social occasion and establishes all sorts of understandings about making choices and talking and listening to one another in a relaxed and pleasant environment, where time has been taken to make sure that the tableware, cutlery and linen contribute to a sense of worth and well-being on the part of the diners. It also establishes that we belong to a community which values eating as a social activity.

Whether you offer children a small snack or provide full meals, there are opportunities for learning - for developing personal, social, emotional, intellectual and language skills, along with independence and a strong sense of self-worth and capability.

What do you want children to learn?

Eating food is not just about satisfying hunger - there is much learning which

can take place, some good and some bad. Your children can learn how to make healthy choices or unhealthy ones; they can learn that they are capable and have many skills, such as pouring liquid from a jug, or they can learn that they are too unimportant to be allowed the time to learn this vital skill. They can learn that snack times are times for social interaction or for being made to feel powerless and uninvolved in their own care. The choice is yours because you are the adult and can choose to empower the children in your care.

The principles of the *Curriculum Guidance for the Foundation Stage* encourage practitioners to support

Messages in *Birth to Three Matters*

Birth to Three Matters supports an approach to mealtimes which develops children's independence and sense of self-worth.

The 'Making Meaning' aspect of 'A Skilful Communicator', for instance, asks practitioners to 'Respect young children's choices'.

'Healthy Choices' in 'A Healthy Child' encourages you to 'Discuss options so that children really do have choices; for example whether they will drink water, juice or milk', while 'Growing and Developing' in the same aspect urges you to 'Support, supervise and become involved as babies and children try out their developing skills', such as pouring their own choice of drink or spooning their own food onto their plates.

children in making choices and developing their independence.

Because children don't learn skills in isolation, and because skills learned in one area are likely to be used in quite a different context when needed, it is perfectly possible to address aspects of all six areas of the curriculum in any snack or mealtime.

- Offering a choice of snack and allowing children to choose when they have it is developing a child's sense of self-esteem.

- Interacting with others, negotiating and taking turns in conversation happens naturally over food. Communicating likes and dislikes, asking to swap places, and asking questions about the food available will develop skills in oracy. Writing or drawing menus on boards or sheets of paper will develop literacy.

- Opportunities to use mathematical language will occur when sandwiches are cut into different shapes. Counting and matching the pieces of fruit needed to give everybody a piece, and then cutting the fruit, makes the need for accuracy clear. Using positional language to help lay the table is another way to take any opportunity to develop concepts in maths.

- Children need to be aware that a healthy diet is a varied one, that lots of recipes from other cultures are healthy, and that traditional English food is not the only food available to us.

- Physical skills of dexterity are developed by practising pouring, cutting and moving food and drink using appropriate tools and containers.

- To develop children's sensory awareness, they need to know the language of taste – words such as 'salty', 'sweet', 'fruity', 'spicy', 'sour' and 'bitter'. They also need to have the opportunity to experience all these flavours and talk about them.

- Children need to be creative in their approach to food, exploring colour and texture with their sense of taste and their senses of sight and smell.

Your role

The role of the adult is crucial in making meal and snack times into a significant event which enhances independence and learning for children.

Many adults have strong views about food, often linked to the concept of waste. Some adults have been brought up with an attitude to food which links it to behaviour management, in other words 'If you eat all your dinner you can have your sweet/pudding/ chocolate biscuit'. Using food, including sweets, lollipops or even fruit as a reward for good behaviour is engrained in our culture but should be avoided if at all possible.

Using food to exert power over children can lead to them getting this message clearly and using it in their turn to exert power over adults. In its extreme form, it can lead to bulimia and anorexia, but can also lead to faddy eating habits, such as the child who will only eat fish finger or only ever eat one type of chocolate biscuit. They can then have a controlling effect on parents, who will often buy only what their child will eat because they can't face the uproar that the child will make otherwise.

The question we need to ask is why some children feel the need to behave in this way. Is it because they have no other way of expressing their opinions and making the adults around them listen to what they are trying to say? Such behaviour is a cry for help, a cry for their voice to be heard and their wants and needs to be taken into account in all areas which affect them.

Listening to children – really listening to what they have to say, their opinions and their understanding of what is happening around them - is what the role of the adult should be at mealtimes and snack times. If children know that you will listen to what they have to say and share their thinking process, you will be able to make the most of any learning experiences which present themselves at mealtimes.

Manners – socially acceptable behaviour for everyone

You have a crucial role in showing children the importance of good manners by providing a good role

'Eating out is a social occasion and establishes all sorts of understandings about making choices and talking and listening to one another in a relaxed and pleasant environment.'

model in your interactions with other adults and with children in the setting.

Children learn by imitation far more than by being told about something. Yes, of course we should help children to understand the importance of good social interaction, and the effects that it has on relationships, making communication easier and smoothing the path for future interactions between people. Of course, saying 'please' and 'thank you' is an important skill to learn. However, this is a two-way process with the greater responsibility lying with the adults involved.

Chris Heald is quality assurance co-ordinator and advisory teacher for the Early Years Development and Childcare Partnership in Bury, Lancashire.

Preparing and eating food together

Eating is fundamental to existence and should be enjoyable. It means happy social occasions and family life. Alison Fawcett feels passionately about food and eating. Here she explains why food should be respected and why, as child carers, we must help children to understand this

Many of us have forgotten the importance of food. We say we haven't time to bake or prepare food – and this attitude is passed on to our children. As child carers it is imperative that we make food preparation and meal times fun and fulfilling. We need to include the children and provide them with positive role models.

Many factors dictate what we eat – money, availability, season, diet, peer group pressure, advertising, transport, fads, health needs and

allergies, education and culture to name a few, but I feel we need to take a leaf out of the French's book. They eat food 'of the region', sit at large family tables and spend time relaxing and eating with their families and friends.

Fewer people in this country have dining tables where they can all sit. Emphasis is placed on speed and pre-prepared and microwaveable meals are common in the supermarkets. Meals are eaten while watching television. (Roald Dahl captures this theme well in *Matilda* - perhaps that could be a good starting point for a discussion with the children in your care!)

> It doesn't matter how old we are or what sex we are, we all learn more by doing than by watching.
>
> 'When I see I forget. When I hear I remember. When I do I understand.' (Chinese proverb)

Our eating habits are inherited from a wide range of sources. There would be no common answer to 'What do the British eat for Sunday dinner?' So, what can child carers do to make food interesting and significant?

What you can do

■ Get children to sit down together for their snacks and meals.

■ Make the table a welcoming and comfortable place to be. Clear everything off the table apart from things required for the meal. Cover it with a colourful plastic covering or individual mats that can be easily wiped and cleaned.

■ Have a ready supply of serviettes (get the economy ones) or kitchen roll on or near the table.

■ Include the children in their high chairs. Pull them up to the table and make them part of the group. Don't leave them in the corner!

■ Make eating a social occasion – encourage children to talk about things of interest to them.

■ Encourage children to try new things. Introduce them gradually – if you are trying new fruits, get them to predict what they might taste like; what the inside might look like and whether it is good for them.

■ Encourage children to take the quantity of food that they want. This can be done by putting food on communal plates and offering and sharing it around. Reassure children that there will be more if they want to take a little at first. Be patient. They will develop their skills with practice!

- Encourage children to wait until everyone has finished. There is no harm in them sitting with an empty plate for a while. By doing this you prevent children from deliberately finishing first so that they can get the best seat or favourite toy.

- Emphasise that food is the energy source for their bodies, perhaps introducing an analogy of engines and fuel. The further an engine travels the more fuel it needs. The same goes for children - the more energetic they are the more fuel they need.

What to eat

- Involve children in choosing what they eat.

- Make an activity of going to the shops specifically to buy the food for lunch or tea. If you live near the shops, walk there and let children share the responsibility of carrying their food back in sensibly sized bags.

- Make sure that you know all the children's allergies. Check with the parents that the allergies are just that and not dislikes.

- Let all the children join in the preparation - with supervision they can help with many things. Talk to them about basic hygiene - the importance of washing hands before preparing food; safe use of knives; keeping cooked and fresh meat apart; covering stored food for freshness and being aware of sell-by and use-by dates.

- Let children prepare realistic menus. Some children do not like writing but enjoy sticking or colouring. Make them fun. Save them in a display folder and use them again. Give children guidance on balanced meals. Perhaps you could all invent a simple shopping or eating game.

- Always make sure that there is a jug of water handy for children to help themselves from.

- Remember that food the children prepare themselves is often much more appetising to them! Making lunch can be a full and rewarding morning's occupation for a group of younger children.

Keeping to a budget

With older children it is fun to let them budget for a meal. If it is impossible to do it with a real budget, let them do it with a notional budget. Say that there is £X allocated for lunch and put stickers on different foods to represent their cost - these could be coloured to represent 50p, £1, £2 and so on. It would not take much preparation to mark up things like eggs, cheese, tuna, bread, fruit and salad.

Get different products out and talk children through the costs. Older children might be interested to look on tins and packets to see where goods come from. Place names could be looked up on maps. You can discuss the cost of transporting goods into the country.

Growing food

Children love watching things grow. Runner bean seeds are intriguing because they grow so fast. Mustard and cress can also be grown quickly on wet kitchen roll or (more excitingly) on the top of a potato to make a potato head with hair.

Courgettes are easy to grow in an outside container and produce satisfyingly large vegetables quickly.

Ginger root and garlic cloves can be planted with satisfying results as can sunflowers. If you manage to grow sunflowers successfully you can use the seed heads to feed the birds in winter.

Baking

Children love baking their own buns. They are easy and tasty, particularly when they are fresh out of the oven. Get children to pick the sort of things that they like in their buns, for example sultanas, cherries, raisins, chocolate drops, sunflower seeds, caraway and coconut. Include them all in the measuring and mixing and then allow them to spoon the mixture into the cases. A child in a high chair can easily be given a bun case to place something like raisins in.

All children love making dough. If you do not want to wait too long for the activity you can buy packet bread/pizza mix and have it part prepared before children arrive. They can then pummel and stretch their dough and make it to the shape they want. Bread hedgehogs are always popular - just get a pair of blunt (and clean) scissors and snip vs into an oval of dough. Make a snout and you have hedgehog bread rolls. Even toddlers can join in this. Make sure that the dough does not get in their mouths.

Remember to show your enthusiasm for food by example. Make food preparation all inclusive and enjoyable and remember to follow your daily table routine. Most importantly, make time for eating snacks and meals together in a happy and relaxed atmosphere.

Alison Fawcett, childcare tutor, Sheffield.

Learning from cooking

Recipe for learning: Fruit kebabs

This recipe combines healthy eating and lots of learning opportunities. The process is simple so children can be actively involved most of the time. Take advantage of the abundance of fruits available at this time of year – and get cooking!

Try to work with groups of no more than four children.

Ingredients
Choose 4-6 of the following:
1 eating apple, cored
1 firm pear, cored
1 firm banana
8 large prunes, stoned
2 fresh or dried figs
2 slices of pineapple, fresh or canned
1 firm peach
2 apricots, stoned

Coating:
Grated rind and juice of 1 lemon
2 tablespoons of maple syrup
2 tablespoons of hazelnut or walnut oil
bamboo skewer

Heat the grill to a medium temperature

Note: Be careful with the skewers – children may be tempted to use them for an impromptu sword fight!

What to do
Step 1: Put the fruit on a plate and ask children to choose which they would like to try on their kebab.

Suggest a certain number, for example four fruits. Display the number four beside the plate so that the children come to recognise it in context.

Step 2: Prepare the fruit for the kebab.

Under careful supervision, help children use a sharp knife to cut their fruit. Cut the banana into four pieces, quarter the apples and pears, halfve the apricots, figs and peaches, and cut the pineapple into small chunks. Count aloud as each piece of fruit is cut and use language such as 'quarters' and 'halves'.

Step 3: Prepare the coating.

Mix together the lemon juice and rind, the walnut or hazelnut oil and the maple syrup. Children can pour each ingredient into a separate cup or small bowl and then add all three liquids together in one big bowl at the end. This way if they pour too much into their cup you can take some out without spoiling the whole mixture. Use language such as 'too much' and 'take away'. Count the spoonfuls added aloud.

Step 4: Cover each fruit in the coating.

Help children to cover all their fruit with the coating. They will need to dip their fingers in the mixture. How does it feel? Sticky? Cold? What does it smell like? Encourage children to use their senses.

Step 5: Thread the fruit onto the skewers.

Help children to put the skewer through the middle of the fruit. Controlling the skewer is a similar skill to holding a pencil as it uses the same pincer grip. If the pieces are small enough, try to repeat the pattern of fruit threaded, for example, banana, fig, apple, prune, banana, fig, apple, prune.

If you only use two fruits, you could repeat the pattern several times over, for example, pear, apricot, pear, apricot, pear, apricot.

Step 6: Place the kebabs under a pre-heated grill for two or three minutes until browned, then carefully turn them over and brown on the other side.

Give children a one-minute sand timer. Ask them to tell you when they have turned it over twice and all the sand has run out. That is your cue to turn the kebabs over.

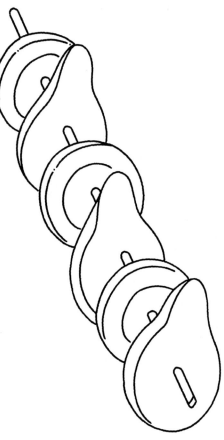

Show children the side which has been cooked and compare it to the side which has not been cooked. Ask them to notice any differences.

Put the uncooked kebab under the grill and ask children to turn the sand timer over two more times.

Step 7: Leave the kebabs to cool a little before serving with Greek yoghurt or crème fraiche.

While children are waiting for the kebabs to cool, they can help to clear up by wiping the table and washing up the utensils, leaving the sharp knives to the adults. Show them how to stack plates and how to turn cups and bowls upside down so that the water drains away.

■ If preferred, you can grill the fruits without coating them first: they won't look as shiny and will taste less sweet, but will have the benefit of no added sugar.

Nicola Stobbs, early years teacher, Rushwick Pre-School, Worcester.

Choose from the following:

 1 cored eating apple

 1 cored pear

 1 banana

 8 stoned prunes

 2 figs

 2 slices of pineapple

 1 stoned peach

 2 stoned apricots

Coating:

 Grated rind and juice of one lemon

 2 tablespoons of maple syrup

 2 tablespoons of hazelnut or walnut oil

 bamboo skewers

1. Turn on the grill. Choose some fruit that you would like to try in your kebab.

2. Prepare the fruit. Choose some fruit and cut into bite sized chunks.

3. Make the coating. Mix together the lemon juice, hazel or walnut oil and maple syrup.

4. Cover each fruit in the coating- you will have to use your fingers!

5. Thread the fruit onto the skewers. Try to put the skewer straight through the middle and make a pattern with your fruit.

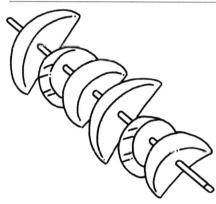

6. Put the kebabs under the grill. Turn the sand timer over as you count how long they will take to cook. Turn them over twice.

7. Leave the kebabs to cool before serving with Greek yoghurt or crème fraiche. Remember to clean up!

If you don't like the fruit heated then you can eat it without the coating and grilling.

Cooking provides valuable lessons not just about weighing and measuring but also about breaking a task down into the stages that must be performed in a sequence; a valuable skill needed when learning to read, and one which does not come naturally to children.

Recipe for learning: Minestrone soup

This soup is great for autumn. Both the beans and the pasta provide slow release energy that will sustain children for longer before they need to eat again. It is also full of vegetables readily available at this time of year, which you will find children are happy to eat because they have made the soup themselves

> Try to work with groups of no more than four children.

Ingredients

1 tablespoon olive oil
1 leek
1 garlic clove
2 carrots
1 stick celery
170ml (2.5 pints) water
2 oz pastina (tiny pasta shapes)
125g (4oz) Savoy cabbage, sprouts or any other leafy green vegetable
425g (14oz) can of flageolet or cannelloni beans
4 fresh basil leaves
squeeze of lemon
salt (optional) and black pepper

1 teaspoon, 1 tablespoon, 1 wooden spoon
cup/bowl
minute sand timer
measuring jug
large saucepan

What to do

Step 1: Put all the ingredients on a plate.

Refer to the recipe card (overleaf) and ask children to help you name each ingredient in the pictures and compare it to the real ingredient. They could pick up each one and describe it, for example, they may notice that the leek and celery have lines along them or that the sprouts and cabbage have leaves.

Ask children where vegetables come from. Some may have helped to harvest vegetables in their own gardens.

Step 2: Prepare the vegetables.

Ask children to choose a vegetable. Explain that because vegetables grow in the ground they must be washed before eating. Show them how to wash their vegetable in a bowl of cold water and dry it on a piece of kitchen roll. Under careful supervision, help children use a

sharp knife to cut it into small slices; the carrots will need to be peeled, so help children learn to use a vegetable peeler. Count aloud as each piece of vegetable is cut.

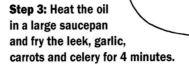

Step 3: Heat the oil in a large saucepan and fry the leek, garlic, carrots and celery for 4 minutes.

Ask a child to find the biggest metal spoon on the table (the tablespoon). Compare it to the teaspoon and wooden spoon. Talk about the sizes and functions of each spoon. Have children pour the olive oil onto the tablespoon over a small cup or bowl to catch any spillages.

Explain that the vegetables need to cook for four minutes. Use a minute sand timer and ask children to turn it over four times. Display the number four so that children associate the number with an amount of time.

Note: Saucepan handles should always face away from children as they could get caught in clothing.

Step 4: Pour in the water and bring to the boil. Add the pasta and simmer, covered, for 5 minutes.

Use a jug with a sticker on the 750ml line. Ask children to pour the water into the jug, stopping when the water reaches the level of the sticker. Encourage language such as 'too much' and 'take away'. Children can pour the water into the pot. Explain that you are going to make it very hot. They will know when the water is boiling because there will be steam coming out of the pot. Tell them that they should never go near a boiling pot.

Look at the dry pasta shapes. Ask them if they can predict how the texture will change after it is cooked. Pour the shapes into the cup. An adult should then add the pasta to the boiling water.

Step 5: Add the cabbage or other greens and simmer for a further 5 minutes.

Ask children to sort the ingredients so that all the green vegetables are ready to go in the pot. An adult should then add them to the other ingredients.

When adding the herbs, compare the fresh basil leaves to dried ones. Explain that this is how the basil leaves look after they have been dried. Drying makes them last longer.

Step 6: Add the tomatoes, beans and pepper. Stir in the herbs, lemon juice and a little salt (if using). Cook for a further 2 minutes until heated through.

Explain that the tomatoes and beans once grew on plants just like the other vegetables but have been put into cans in a factory. This makes them last a long time.

Squeezing the lemon will build muscles in the hands necessary for fine motor control. Once squeezed, add it to the soup with the salt and pepper.

While children are waiting for the soup to cool, they can wipe the table and wash up utensils, leaving sharp knives to the adults. Show how to stack plates and how to turn cups and bowls upside down so that the water drains away.

If preferred, you can liquidise the soup and add the pastina later.

Nicola Stobbs, early years teacher, Rushwick Pre-School, Worcester.

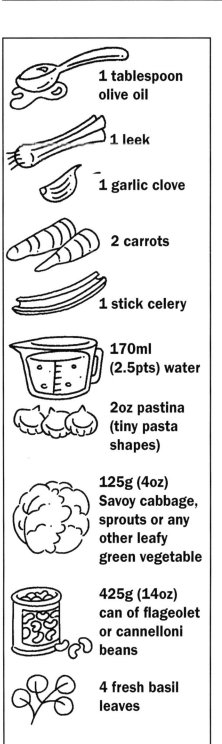

	1 tablespoon olive oil
	1 leek
	1 garlic clove
	2 carrots
	1 stick celery
	170ml (2.5pts) water
	2oz pastina (tiny pasta shapes)
	125g (4oz) Savoy cabbage, sprouts or any other leafy green vegetable
	425g (14oz) can of flageolet or cannelloni beans
	4 fresh basil leaves
	squeeze of lemon
	salt and black pepper

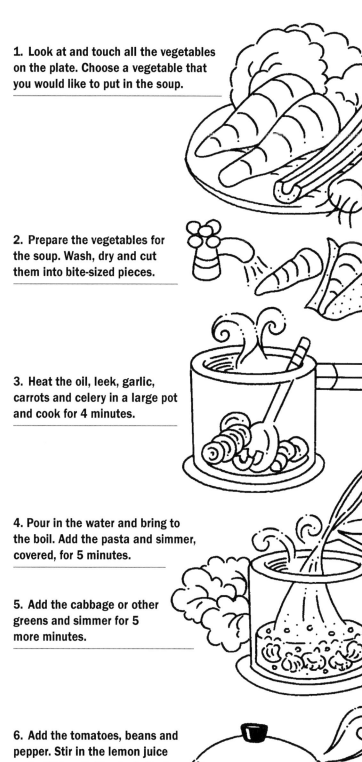

1. Look at and touch all the vegetables on the plate. Choose a vegetable that you would like to put in the soup.

2. Prepare the vegetables for the soup. Wash, dry and cut them into bite-sized pieces.

3. Heat the oil, leek, garlic, carrots and celery in a large pot and cook for 4 minutes.

4. Pour in the water and bring to the boil. Add the pasta and simmer, covered, for 5 minutes.

5. Add the cabbage or other greens and simmer for 5 more minutes.

6. Add the tomatoes, beans and pepper. Stir in the lemon juice and a little salt (if using). Cook for a further 2 minutes until heated through. Don't forget to clean up!

If you don't like the lumps in the soup, then you can ask an adult to liquidise it.

Recipe for learning:
Cheese and tomato kites

Cooking with children can be messy and stressful, yet the learning opportunities are so great that it's worth making the effort. Nicola Stobbs' recipe page comes complete with a recipe sheet to copy and laminate for children. She includes points to discuss along the way

Try to work with groups of no more than four children.

Ingredients
Makes six tarts

375g (13oz) packet of ready-rolled puff pastry
1 tablespoon milk
1 tube of tomato puree
dried herbs
225g (8oz) cherry tomatoes
225g (8oz) mozzarella cheese
100g (4oz) mushrooms
1 pepperoni sausage
1 red pepper
watercress with leaves removed for string

Heat oven to 220 degrees C, 425 degrees F, gas mark 7.

What to do

Step 1: Turn on the oven. Unroll the pastry, divide it into six pieces, and put it on a baking sheet.

Ask children if they know what shape the pastry is. Tell them that you want to divide it into six pieces. Can they think of a way? To help them, score the pastry into three strips. Start to divide each strip in half, counting each one as you do. Give one child a knife and, under careful supervision, let them cut the pastry where you have scored. Let the other children have a go and continue until all six pieces are cut out. Give each child a piece of pastry on a plate.

Step 2: Put the milk into a cup. Use a pastry brush to brush the milk around the edges of the pastry.

Help children to hold the pastry brush as if it were a pencil in the pincer grip. Children who may not show any interest in writing or painting on paper may feel more confident about mark making in this situation.

Step 3: Let children squeeze a teaspoon of tomato puree onto the pastry. Spread it around thinly but not over the milky border.

Squeezing a tube of puree will help build muscles in children's hands. Using the knife to spread the puree is also part of this muscle development and control. Use language such as 'thinly' to describe how to spread so that children hear this difficult word in context.

Step 4: Put some dried mixed herbs onto a saucer and let children sprinkle a few herbs onto their pastry.

Help children to control the amount of herbs they use by saying 'too much' or 'a little bit more'. Point out any spaces they have left bare to reinforce the concept of space. The motion of sprinkling the herbs is made by holding the fingers in the pincer movement, the same one needed for holding a pencil.

Step 5: Use a serrated knife to cut the tomatoes in half. Cut the pepperoni sausage into thin slices; the pepper and the mushrooms into pieces. Add them to the pastry.

Suggest amounts of each ingredient to add, for example, can the children add three tomatoes and three pepperoni sausages? One slice of mushroom and two peppers? Encourage children to count out aloud as they put them onto the pastry. Counting in this way teaches one to one correspondence in its most practical way.

Step 6: Open the bag of cheese and pour away any liquid. Cut into 1cm cubes. Spread evenly over the pastry.

To help children cut the cheese into 1cm cubes, firstly cut it yourself into 1cm thick strips. Show them how to make little cubes. Use the word 'cube' as often as you can and, if appropriate, discuss their properties. Ask children to put an equal number of cubes onto their pastry; four or six, depending on the size of the pastry. Again, count aloud together as you add the cubes.

Step 7: Put the pastry back onto a baking sheet and place on the middle shelf of the oven for 25-30 minutes, until the pastry rises and turns brown.

Point out that the pastry kites are on the middle shelf, to reinforce positional language. Set a timer for 25 minutes that will ping when the tarts are ready to reinforce the concept of time.

Step 8: Leave the tarts on the baking sheet for about three minutes to cool. Then serve, decorating with the watercress string.

Show children how the pastry has changed after cooking. Can they see how it is now brown and has risen where the milk was brushed? What do they notice about the cheese? The shape which was once a square has become the shape of a kite.

Nicola Stobbs, early years teacher, Rushwick Pre-School, near Worcester.

Makes 6 tarts

 puff pastry

 1 tablespoon milk

 tomato puree

 dried herbs

 1 cup of cherry tomatoes

 1 cup of mozzarella cheese

 1/2 cup of mushrooms

 1 pepperoni sausage

 1 red pepper

 watercress with leaves removed to look like string

1: Turn on the oven.Unroll the pastry and cut into 6.

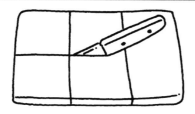

2: Brush milk around the edge of each piece.

3: Squeeze 1 teaspoon of tomato puree onto the pastry. Spread it around but not over the milk.

4: Sprinkle some dried herbs onto the pastry.

5: Cut the tomatoes in half. Cut the pepperoni sausage into thin slices and the pepper and mushrooms into pieces. Put them on the pastry.

6: Cut the cheese into 1cm cubes. Spread over the pastry.

7: Put the pastry on a baking sheet and place onto the middle shelf of the oven for 25-30 minutes, until the pastry rises and turns brown.

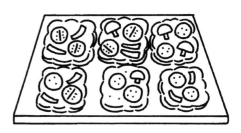

8: Leave the tarts on the baking sheet for 3 minutes to cool. Serve with the watercress string.

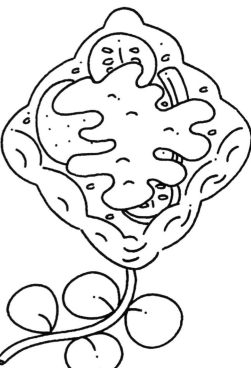

Promoting healthy eating

The Government guidelines on healthy eating were drawn up as a direct result of disease patterns within the population. Too many of us are suffering from heart disease, diabetes, cancer, high blood pressure, strokes and obesity. Many of these diseases are on the increase.

'The balance of good health' is a visual representation – a picture of a plate of food – used by the Food Standards Agency to show the recommended proportions of foods that we should be eating, not necessarily on a daily basis, but over a period of time. The message is clear that we need to make fruit and vegetables and starchy foods, which include bread, potatoes, pasta, rice and other cereals, the main part of our diet. The high fat, high sugar section at the bottom of the plate is a clear acknowledgement that these foods are a part of everybody's diet. That the portion is small clearly demonstrates that they need to be kept to a minimum.

The balance of good health is based on the eight guidelines for a healthy diet which are:

- enjoy your food

- eat a variety of different foods

- eat the right amount to be a healthy weight

- eat plenty of foods rich in starch and fibre

- eat plenty of fruit and vegetables

- don't eat too many foods that contain a lot of fat

- don't have sugary foods and drinks too often

- if you drink alcohol do it in moderation.

But does all of this apply to children and at what age do the guidelines start to apply? Growing children need plenty of energy (calories) and nutrients to ensure that they grow and develop well. A good appetite will usually mean that they get enough energy from the food that they eat.

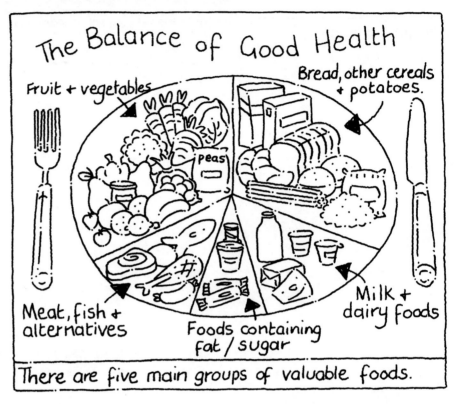

The Balance of Good Health

Fruit + vegetables

Bread, other cereals + potatoes.

peas

Meat, fish + alternatives

Foods containing fat / sugar

Milk + dairy foods

There are five main groups of valuable foods.

There is, however, increasing evidence of poor diet in children. The National Diet and Nutrition Survey of young people aged 4 to 18 published in 2000 found:

- Only 60% of boys and 40% of girls meet the Health Education Authority recommendation for at least half an hour of moderate activity per day (e.g. brisk walking)

- On average British children are eating less than half the recommended five portions of fruit and vegetables per day. The study demonstrates regional and economic differenced, particularly with fruit and vegetable intake

- Evidence from blood samples of poor nutritional status with regard to iron and some vitamin B samples. A substantial number of children had low blood levels of vitamin D, particularly during the winter months.

- A national survey in 1995 showed that children's diets are too high in sugar (17 per cent of children aged 18 months to four and a half years have some form of tooth decay).

Obesity, and a particular type of diabetes related to obesity, is increasing in children. Children are less active than in previous generations, spending more time watching television and playing outside less, hence they have lower energy requirements.

Four main food groups
Clearly there are significant nutritional challenges facing children and their carers, but the balance of good health still applies to this group and you can use it as a basis for encouraging children to eat a varied diet. They should eat foods from four main food groups every day.

These food groups are:

- bread, other cereals and potatoes

- fruits and vegetables

- milk and dairy foods

- meat, fish, eggs and alternatives such as beans, lentils and soya.

Bread, other cereals and potatoes
Whether it is bread, breakfast cereals, maize, potatoes, yams, rice, couscous, pasta or chapattis, most children don't need much encouragement to eat one

or more of the foods from this group. A portion at each meal will provide energy, various nutrients and some fibre. Ideally, children should try lots of different varieties of starchy foods, such as wholemeal bread as well as white.

Potatoes are a useful source of vitamin C. Boil or mash them – or occasionally try chips. Thick straight cut chips have less fat or choose lower fat oven chips. Limit fried potato to once or twice a week.

Starchy foods are important in everyone's diet but they can be filling. This is especially true of wholemeal varieties. Be careful not to use too many wholemeal foods until the child is five. For fussy eaters, children with small appetites and children who are thin or slow growers use wholemeal varieties with caution after this age also. Of course, the reverse is true for children who are overweight, the wholemeal varieties are then very useful.

Toast, cereals and teacakes make useful snacks. They are more nutritious than biscuits and crisps and can often work out cheaper, too.

Fruit and vegetables
Fruit and vegetables contain vitamins, minerals and fibre and they liven up meals with colour, textures and flavours. Try to introduce lots of them from an early age, whether fresh, frozen, canned or dried.

The adult recommendation is to eat five portions from this group each day, one portion being an apple, a banana, a tablespoon of carrots, one or two florets of broccoli, and so on. Children should also aim for about five portions, but clearly not the same portion size. Try to give children a taste of five different fruits and vegetables each day. The amount that they will eat of each will vary from child to child depending on appetite, age preference, and so on.

When children flatly refuse vegetables, keep offering them but also offer more fruit. Make sure you show that you like eating them. It's counter productive to make a big fuss if children refuse, but remember, between the ages of one and five, all children should receive vitamin drops unless a wide variety of food is being eaten. Healthy Start vitamin supplements replace the Welfare Vitamins. Children's drops contain vitamins A, C and D. The Healthy Start scheme is open to pregnant women (from 10 weeks) and children under 4 years old in families on Income Support, income-based Job Seeker's Allowance and Child Tax Credit (without working tax credit) and an annual income of £14,155 or less. It is also open to all pregnant women under 18 years of age. NHS clinics remain responsible for stocking and distributing vitamin supplements.

Try some of the following:

- For snacks, try sticks of carrot, cucumber and celery; sliced apple, banana or pear; cherry tomatoes, sugar snaps or mange tout. Some children also like sliced raw mushroom or raw baby sweetcorn.

- Children's cooking sessions often generate interest in food so try to base these on healthy options. Get them to pile vegetables or pineapple onto pizza bases. They're much more likely to eat them if they've had a hand in the preparation.

- Try out some fruit art, making smiley faces with fruit and vegetables.

- Use a colourful display of fruit and vegetables as inspiration for paintings.

Milk and dairy foods
Milk is important for young children. A minimum of half a pint of milk each day will provide energy for growth and calcium for bones and teeth.

Semi-skimmed milk can be introduced from two years of age. However, fussy eaters, children who are thin or those who have a large intake of milk and seem to be dependant on it for a large proportion of their calories are best left on whole milk until they are older. Skimmed milk is not suitable for children under five. Some families and carers will also be eligible for free milk (seven pints per week).

If a child doesn't like drinking milk every day, they need at least two servings of milk-based dishes such as cheese, yoghurt, fromage frais, custard, milk puddings and cheese sauce. Contrary to popular belief, eggs don't fall into this category; they are not a rich source of calcium.

For children who are allergic to milk or for vegan children (not taking any animal products at all) it is important that they are getting enough calcium as well as some other important nutrients provided by milk. Doctors or health visitors will be able to advise on infant soya milks. For older children make sure you buy rice or soya milk with added calcium.

Some children may be referred by their doctor to a dietician who will be able to check if the child's diet is adequate.

Meat, fish, eggs and alternatives

Young children need protein to grow and develop. Meat, fish, eggs, nuts, pulses (beans, lentils, and peas), foods made from pulses (tofu, hummus, soya mince) and Quorn are an excellent source of protein. Children need at least one portion from this group each day.

For children who are vegetarian or vegan two portions of vegetable proteins (pulses) or nuts daily will ensure they receive enough protein. Whole nuts should not be given to children under five years of age, as there is a risk of choking. Allergy to nuts appears to be on the increase. If you suspect an allergy, avoid that food and check with the parent or main carer.

Fats and sugars

The fifth main food group covers foods that are high in fat and/ or sugar.

Foods such as crisps, chips, biscuits, chocolate, cakes and fried foods are high in fat. They provide relatively little else in terms of useful nutrients. They are often popular with children as well as adults! All of these foods need to be limited. Have a look at the balance of good health and remember they can be a part of a healthy diet, as long as they are only a small part.

Breast milk is quite sweet and children continue to like sweet tastes. The total amount of sugar needs to be limited in children's diets, but even more important is how often they are taking sugar, sugary foods and drinks. When teeth are in frequent contact with sugary foods and drinks they will decay. To reduce the amount of sugar in a child's diet, try setting a precedent and only serve milk and water. This will reduce the total amount of sugar in a child's diet and reduce the frequency of sugar intake.

Alternatively, only serve flavoured drinks at meal times, as this limits the damage done to teeth.

Finally, keep a balance on food. Remember, there are no healthy or unhealthy foods just healthy and unhealthy diets. Food is there to be enjoyed, in as much variety as possible, by children and adults alike.

Beverley Spicer, community paediatric dietician.

Healthy eating schemes

Planning your own healthy eating week or project is always useful, but it's a good idea to have an idea of what is happening elsewhere in your local area and nationally. When your health event coincides with a national event there may be press coverage to support whatever you are trying to achieve, and this will improve the impact of your work.

There are an ever increasing number of schemes funded by the Government, and independent organizations and charities that aim to improve the health of children, and many of them are aimed at combating health inequality. There is a wealth of information that demonstrates clearly the relationship between poverty and health. For example, the death rate of unskilled men is now three times higher than in professional men. Research has also shown that socioeconomic environment in childhood is a useful predictor of cardiovascular disease in adulthood. People in low-income groups eat fewer fruits and vegetables. Their children are about 50 per cent less likely to eat fruit and vegetables than those in high income families. In addition, poorly nourished children, particularly those who are overweight or obese, often experience significant social and psychological problems.

The government schemes which specifically aim to improve the health of children are:

- Sure Start

- Healthy Start

- The School Fruit and Vegetable Scheme

Sure Start

Sure Start is a Government programme, operating in England only. It aims to achieve better outcomes for children, parents and communities by:

- Increasing the availability of childcare for all children

- Improving health and emotional development of young children

- Supporting parents as parents and in their aspirations toward employment

To do this they are:

- Helping services development in disadvantaged areas alongside financial help for parents to afford childcare

- Rolling out the principles driving the Sure Start approach to all services for children and parents

Sure Start acknowledges "diet and nutrition are fundamental to health throughout life. A good diet can help reduce the risk of a number of health problems including obesity, heart disease, some cancers and type 2 diabetes."

Sure Start aims to encourage parents, carers and early year's practitioners to inform themselves on how to give children the healthiest start in life. In addition from April 2008 local authorities will have to conduct Childcare sufficiency assessments and will have a duty to secure sufficient childcare for parents in their area. This in combination with nutrition guidelines for under 5's and the impact of OFSTED inspections to survey registered day care will serve to ensure an adequate supply of pre-school care providing quality food provision, age appropriate nutrition and introducing children to a good diet whatever their prior home experience.

Every Child Matters is linked with Sure Start. The "Every child matters" report (Department for Education and Skills, 2003), introduced a new focus on quality services for children in the UK.

The Government's aim is for every child, whatever their background or their circumstances, to have the support they need to:

- Be healthy

- Stay safe

- Enjoy and achieve

- Make a positive contribution

- Achieve economic wellbeing

This means that the organizations involved with providing services to children – from hospitals and schools, to police and voluntary groups – will be teaming up in new ways to help achieve children achieve what they want from life.

The health aspect of Every Child Matters is linked with Standard 8 of the

children under 4 years old in families on Income Support, income-based Job Seeker's Allowance and Child Tax Credit (without working tax credit) and an annual income of £14,155 or less. It is also open to all pregnant women under 18 years of age.

Pregnant women and children over one and under five will receive one voucher per week, worth £2.80, for each child or pregnancy. Children under one year old will receive two vouchers per child, worth a total of £5.60. The value of the vouchers will be adjusted periodically to ensure they continue to keep pace with the retail prices of milk, fruit and vegetables and infant formula.

Retailers who sell any of the Healthy Start foods can apply to register as a Healthy Start food outlet. They can be recognized by a red and green sticker saying "Healthy Start Vouchers welcome here". All of the big supermarkets are signed up, as are some local retailers. Local retailers can be found by postcode on the website.

More information on the new scheme is available on the Healthy Start website www.healthystart.nhs.uk

The School Fruit and Vegetable Scheme

Funded by the Department of Health, this is part of the 5-A-Day programme to increase fruit and vegetable consumption. The scheme entitles all four to six year old children in Local Education Authority (LEA)-maintained infant, primary and special schools to a free piece of fruit or vegetable each school day.

Rickets is a deficiency of vitamin D. Vitamin D is made in the body when we are exposed to sunlight. However, there is only sufficient sunlight in the UK, during the summer months. Rickets is most often found in people with dark skins, in particular those of Asian and African Caribbean background. The skin pigmentation reduces the body's ability to make vitamin D. This is compounded if culture dictates that the body is covered extensively when outside. Rickets is entirely preventable by taking the Healthy Start vitamins on a daily basis. Previous supply problems with Welfare Vitamins resulted in a disruption to this scheme. Asking whether your children or pregnant mums receive vitamins and letting know where to obtain them free of charge is simple and would potentially prevent this painful and disfiguring disease. You really can make a difference.

National Service Framework (NSF) for Children, Young People and Maternity Services.

For more information visit www.surestart.gov.uk. This website provides an extensive number of links to other sites providing support and information on good nutrition and healthy eating for women and children.

Healthy Start (Replaces the Welfare Food Scheme)

The current Welfare Food Scheme was introduced in Britain to combat food shortages during the Second World War. It offered milk and infant formula to low income families. Healthy Start

replaces the Welfare Food Scheme.

NHS clinics no longer supply infant formula and do not accept Healthy Start vouchers. NHS clinics remain responsible for stocking and distributing vitamin supplements.

Healthy Start vitamin supplements replace the Welfare Vitamins. Children's drops contain vitamins A, C and D. Women's tablets contain vitamins C, D and folic acid. Rickets* continues to be diagnosed in babies and children in the UK. The continuation of free vitamins to this most vulnerable group is welcomed.

The Healthy Start scheme is open to pregnant women (from 10 weeks) and

Over 500 schools took part in early pilots of the scheme. Findings were encouraging and included:

- 99% of schools thought the reliability of the fruit deliveries was excellent or acceptable

- 93% of schools thought the overall quality of the fruit was good

- The majority of children were positive about the scheme

- 55% of schools noticed an improvement in the ethos and atmosphere in the classes involved in the scheme

The scheme has been evaluated to check on overall success and the perspective of parents and teachers. Parents reported that:

- Over a quarter of children and their families ate more fruit at home after their school joined the scheme.

- Nearly half of the parents questioned think the scheme has made them more aware of the importance of fruit for a healthy diet

- 95% of parents say their child always, often or sometimes ate the fruit provided at school.

Guidance is provided to schools to help introduce the scheme, but schools are free to implement the scheme in the way they think is best for their school.

Healthy eating training

The Pre-school Learning Alliance has launched a new programme of nutritional training for pre-school practitioners. It will be run in conjunction with the British Nutrition Foundation and is part of the Alliance's Feeding Young Imaginations initiative which aims to promote healthy eating in young children across all settings. The scheme will target as many pre-school practitioners as possible within three years, giving them the skills to plan recipes and menus that are nutritionally balanced. For more information ring the PLA on 020 7697 2500.

Beverley Spicer, community paediatric dietician.

Providing food: The challenges

During infancy (from birth to 12 months) the growth rate is relatively fast; during the pre-school period (one to five years) it slows down. However, the nutritional quality of the diet remains tremendously important and has both short- and long-term implications for children's development.

Current health trends

Dental decay

Results from the National Diet and Nutrition Survey (1995) show that almost one in five children (17 per cent) aged between one and four have some form of tooth decay – a clear indication that their diets contain too much sugar. A reduction in both the amount and the frequency of sugar consumption is required to reduce dental disease in this age group.

Sucrose (packet sugar), glucose, fructose (such as in fruit juice) and maltose (from cooked starch) are most damaging to teeth. Lactose (in milk) is less likely to cause decay. Low calorie drinks have acids added as preservatives. The acidic nature of these drinks causes erosion of the tooth enamel. This type of decay is becoming increasingly common in young children. In the 1995 survey nearly 10 per cent of the children studied were reported to have severe erosion of their upper front teeth.

The same survey found that children with dental decay had higher than average intakes of sugar confectionary and soft drinks, such as fruit squashes containing sugar and carbonated drinks (including low calorie carbonated drinks), than those without decay. Among one- to three-year-olds, taking fruit juice or squash to bed was the main dietary factor which highlighted who did and did not have dental decay. Of the children taking juice or squash to bed 26 per cent had tooth decay compared with 12 per cent who took milk. Decay was particularly common among children having sugary drinks from bottles in bed. Drinking from the bottle takes longer, it may even be sipped throughout the night, hence any sugar in the bottle is being reintroduced to the mouth over a long period of time.

Obesity

Obesity is an urgent, growing health epidemic. If current trends in the UK continue, then by 2020, at least 20% of all boys and 33% of all girls will be obese.

According to "Every Child Matters" obesity is one of the biggest public health issues and its prevalence in children and young people is increasing. The government is responding to the year-on-year rise in obesity with a public service agreement (PSA) target, jointly owned by the Department of Health, the Department of Education and Skills and the Department for Culture Media and Sport.

The challenging PSA target is to halt the year-on-year rise in obesity among children under the age of 11 by 2010. This target will be supported by a programme of action to help children and their families have healthy lifestyles. Success will depend upon a concerted, joined-up effort across government. The following cross-government schemes and initiatives will contribute to reducing childhood obesity:

■ Healthy schools Programme

■ Food in Schools programme (information on TeacherNet)

■ School fruit and vegetable scheme (see *Healthy eating schemes* chapter)

■ Physical education, school sport and Club Links Programme (information on TeacherNet)

Reducing obesity is also one of the six overarching priorities in the public health white paper "Choosing Health".

Primary care trusts are currently working with schools as part of the cross-government programme. One element of this work is will be to take weight and height measurements of all children in reception and year 6. These measurements will help PCTs support schools and target resources more effectively.

Overweight and obese children are likely to become overweight and obese adults. This puts them at greater risk from diabetes, high blood pressure, heart disease and joint problems. They are also likely to be teased by their peers. Often adults, too, are insensitive to the feelings of an overweight child. Studies in America have shown that obese children do less well than their peers in exams at a later age, and

often don't attain as high a salary in adulthood.

So, do overweight children eat more than their peers? In the UK, calorie intakes in children aged one to four fell by 20 per cent between 1967 and 1992, yet the number of overweight children rose during the same period. Inactivity, particularly watching television, is predictive of subsequent overweight and obesity in children. The amount of time watching TV by four- to fifteen-year-olds has doubled since the 1960s.

MEND programme

The MEND programme takes children between 7 and 11 and works with them and their families. The programme has been designed over 5 years by leading experts. The programme combines the elements that recent medical research has shown are essential to effectively overcome overweight and obesity:

Mind: understanding and changing unhealthy attitudes and behaviors around food

Exercise: adequate, safe – and above all fun – exercise

Nutrition: enjoyable, practical activities that teach children about healthy eating

Diet: daily meal planning to improve the whole family's diet.

For further information, visit http://www.mendprogramme.org/

So how are providers of child care faring in the quest for healthier children?

OFSTED published "Food for thought; A survey of healthy Eating in registered day care" in March 2006. Its recommendations included that providers should:

■ Gather details about parental and children's preferences and individual children's dietary requirements; and make sure everyone involved in caring knows about these

■ Plan menus carefully to give children a balanced and nutritious diet, using expert advice if possible.

- Promote healthy eating by helping children and their parents to understand the importance of a healthy diet

- Pay attention to the presentation of food so that children are encouraged to try new things.

Ofsted's Director of Early Years, Dorian Bradley said "So much has been said over the last year about school meals, but few people have talked about the food that younger people eat. I'm pleased to say the picture looks rosy. Childcarers, in the main, have embraced the concept of healthy eating and the wider benefits gained from it."

Ofsted found that most providers place a strong emphasis on home cooked nutritious food using fresh ingredients and low levels of salt, sugar and fat.

Thanks to a good knowledge of healthy eating and a proactive approach to providing nutritious meals, 74% of the childminders and 65% of the day care providers inspected for this survey were judged as good or outstanding with regard to providing a healthy diet.

No childminders, and only 4% of day care providers, were judged inadequate. Only a small minority continue to offer sweets, crisps and biscuits.

"Food for thought; A survey of healthy Eating in registered day care" is on the Ofsted website www.ofsted.gov.uk

Dental health can be improved by encouraging sensible drinking and eating

You can do much to encourage sensible drinking in this age group. If children will drink water and/or milk, then support and encourage this as much as possible. For information on free school milk see http://www.schoolmilk.co.uk

Milk is generally popular in this age group, but children may be more resistant to water, particularly if they have become used to the sweet flavour of fruit juices and squashes.

Children may well drink water if they have poured it themselves. Set aside an area with free access to a jug of water and plastic cups. Encourage children to service this area themselves.

It is important that children drink enough during the day. Free access to water and provision of milk will help

here. However, for children who are not drinking despite this you may well have to consider other drinks. The following advice will minimise any damage.

- Limit juices and squashes to set times, for example, meal times and mid-morning and mid-afternoon.

- Make squash very weak and dilute fruit juice one part juice to five parts water (this also makes both a lot cheaper!)

- Tea and coffee are not recommended for pre school children as they reduce the absorption of iron from foods.

- Keep sweet foods for meal times only and serve fruit and low-sugar snacks (toast, scones, teacakes, toasted muffins, cereals, crackers with margarine or cheese spread) between meals.

- Explain to parents and other carers what you are trying to achieve. It will help enormously if you have them on board, too.

Avoiding overweight and obesity in children

- Encourage physical activity. For parents, this may mean limiting the amount of time spent watching television or playing on a computer.

- Encourage walking as a means of transport – you could take part in 'Walk to school' events.

- Encourage physically active games outside. Try holding a sponsored bounce on a bouncy castle.

- Some overweight children may seem to have large appetites and ask for frequent extras. Use the snacks suggested for limiting dental damage, these will also ensure the children don't go short of any nutrients.

Ensuring adequate intakes of nutrients

The Caroline Walker Trust produces an excellent booklet, *Eating well for under-fives in child care*, which gives practical advice on food choice and presentation to encourage healthy eating. It contains three one-week menus. One is a general menu (see box), the other is suitable for vegetarians and the third includes some multicultural choices. Both meet the nutritional needs for an average three-year-old in child care for a full day. One menu is shown above Compare it with your own. Try introducing some of their ideas. A four- to five-year-old will want

– and need – larger portions, as will children who do not drink milk.

You can obtain a copy of the booklet "Eating well for under-fives in child care" for £20.00 from The Caroline Walker Trust. The training materials (including CD ROM) are also priced £20.00 or if buying two together £30.00. The order form can be downloaded from the website www.cwt.org.uk or contact Caroline Walker Trust at 22 Kindersley Way, Abbots Langley, Hertfordshire WD5 0DQ. Telephone: 01923 269902

Beverley Spicer, community paediatric dietician.

An example menu for 1–4 year olds in child care

	Monday	Tuesday	Wednesday	Thursday	Friday
Mid-morning snack eg. at 10.00am	Milk Canned peaches in juice Whole milk yoghurt	Milk Tabbouleh Breadsticks Cherry tomatoes	Milk Vanilla yoghurt eith banana	Milk Finger food selection of: sliced grapes, celery and red pepper	Milk Wholemeal savoury pancakes with butter Apple chunks
Lunch eg. at 12.00–1.00pm Water and diluted fruit juice available	Chicken korma Brown rice Naan bread Fresh fruit salad	Lamb burgers Bubble and squeak Rice pudding with sultanas	Sardines on toast Sliced tomato Milk jelly with mandarins	Vegetable lasagne Mixed salad Stewed apples with custard	Cottage pie Peas Broccoli Rhubarb crumble
Mid-afternoon snack eg. at 3.00pm	Milk Cucumber and carrot sticks Pitta bread Mint and cucumber dip	Milk Popcorn Sliced pear	Milk Wholemeal toast fingers with margarine Apple	Milk Paprika potato wedges Cheese chunks Orange	Milk Fromage frais with pineapple
Tea eg. at 5.00pm Water and diluted fruit juice available	Egg and cress sandwiches Lettuce Cherry tomatoes Banana custard	Tuna and sweetcorn pasta Cucumber Red pepper Fromage frais Satsuma	Savoury omelette Baby jacket potatoes Semolina with pears	Baked beans and white toast squares Yoghurt with dates	Chicken and vegetable couscous Salad Fresh fruit jelly
Drinking water should be available throughout the day.					

Managing mealtimes

Mealtimes with small children can be a battleground or the highlight of the day. How you manage them is important, from the facilities you provide to the routines you establish. As always, the secret is to plan well and lay down firm boundaries

How children eat when they are in your care is up to you. They may want to share a packet of crisps with the dog in front of the telly but mealtimes can be – and should be – a pleasant social occasion. Most children thrive on routine and regular mealtimes help to shape the day.

Three square meals a day?

Breakfast is a moveable feast for most childcarers. Children arrive at different times – some have been fed before they arrive, others need breakfast before they go off to school or playgroup. Your own partner and children may be in early morning panic mode. A running buffet may work best at this time of the day. Be prepared with fruit juice, milk, cereals, croissants, boiled eggs, toast and fruit. Don't forget to eat yourself!

Children coming home from school will need a snack, which younger children can share, and children staying late will need tea or supper before they leave.

Lunchtime may be the best opportunity for you and the children to sit down together for a proper meal. Keep the food simple, for you and the children, and concentrate on making the shared meal a happy, sociable time for all of you.

Make sure the children have something to keep them occupied while you are

What to eat

Always discuss what children eat with their parents. You need to be aware of any food intolerance or allergies and respect parents' religious and cultural dietary requirements and their wishes for children to be brought up vegetarian or vegan.

preparing food – a game or puzzle, or if all else fails, a favourite video. If you have a clingy child who can't be parted from you – or one you daren't let out of your sight - make sure they are sitting down, either in a high chair or at the kitchen table with crayons or a puzzle. Older children can help with simple food preparation and setting the table.

Sitting comfortably

If you have a small baby to bottle-feed, try to stagger mealtimes so that baby is fed first and your hands are free to help older babies and toddlers. Small children must be sitting safely and comfortably in high chairs or in clip-on seats attached to your dining chairs, always with the appropriate safety harness. You will never have more than three children who need spoon feeding at once, and although you only have one pair of hands, multi-tasking is an essential qualification for a childminder!

Encouraging independence

It's often easier, and quicker, to spoon-feed children but not nearly as much fun as letting them do it themselves. Introduce finger foods as early as you can. A small child should never be left alone with food because of the danger of choking, but while one is happily chewing on a rusk or a piece of soft fruit, you can be tempting a younger child with spoonfuls of pureed food or even grabbing a bite of your own sandwich.

Child-sized plastic spoons and forks can soon take the place of fingers and children do need to learn to cut up their own food before they go to school.

Mealtimes are messy

Reducing stress means neither you nor the children having to worry about mess. If children are going to feed themselves, there will always be a stage when more food ends up on the floor than in the child. Eat in the kitchen if you can and be prepared to sweep up afterwards. Children will accept house rules which say no food or drink in the sitting room. If the kitchen won't accommodate you all, use plastic

Health and safety

Health and safety must be your first priority. The kitchen is the most dangerous room in the house and you will need to reduce the risk of accidents to a minimum. Essential precautions are:

- Safety catches on cupboard doors and on the cutlery drawer;

- A guard round the hob;

- Equipment, especially kettles, placed well back on work surfaces with no trailing flexes;

- Keep the floor dry, clean and litter free.

sheeting under the dining table or a large plastic tablecloth for the children to sit on.

You don't want to be worrying about breakages either, so colourful attractive plastic dishes and cups, with lids for little ones, are essential. You also need bibs, preferably with sleeves. In the summer, the whole operation can be moved into the garden – children love picnics and the birds will clear up for you!

Eat it up – it's good for you

Even very young children understand that they are growing bigger all the time – it's one of their main topics of conversation. It's never too soon to talk to them about food being good for them, making them grow and giving them energy.

Provide reluctant or slow eaters with small portions and offer more if they finish – don't confront them with mountains of food they are required to eat up and try to offer a choice of food.

Go on – just try it

You can establish habits of healthy eating which parents will appreciate and which will help ensure the long-term good health of the children. This is best done by example. Younger children and new recruits are much more likely to eat well and try new foods if you all eat together. Parents are often amazed at what their children will eat at their childminder's house that they wouldn't eat at home, but they will copy their friends and try something new. The more different food you can offer a small child before they are one, the better, but one at time in case of adverse reactions.

Feeding babies

If possible, arrange with parents of young babies that they bring a day's supply of bottled formula or expressed milk with them so you just need to warm the bottle. You will need to keep a spare bottle and formula in stock for emergencies.

A liquidiser is an essential piece of equipment when weaning babies. It is well worth cooking and liquidising a batch of baby food and freezing it in portion size bags or jars. If you are liquidising food you have cooked for your family be careful of salt content. Keep some jars of ready-made baby food in the cupboard. It may not be as nutritionally perfect as you can make it, but it is quick! Sometimes, when baby is yelling his head off, an instant jar may save his lungs and your sanity.

Learn as you eat

Mealtimes become much more interesting if the children have been involved in choosing, planning and buying the food they are going to eat. There is lots of potential on a trip to the supermarket for interesting discussion about where food comes from, how it's grown, processed and transported. You may even grow your own fruit and vegetables in an allotment or garden and children can help you plant seeds or water. Even a window box or a grow-bag can provide a crop of delicious tomatoes and egg shell Humpty Dumpties love cress hair.

Use mealtimes to teach good manners. Using a knife and fork correctly and keeping elbows off the table can come later. Concentrate on the basic: eating food off your own plate, not your friend's, not throwing food, saying please and thank you.

And there's just one more rule: do talk while you are eating. Well, perhaps not with your mouth full, but good conversation is part of the pleasure of any meal and children who enjoy mealtimes will develop a healthy attitude to food which will last a lifetime.

Lindy Hardcastle, childminder, Leicestershire.

Eating more fruit and vegetables

Health experts advise eating at least five portions of fruit and vegetables a day to reduce risks of heart disease, stroke and cancer. But some children turn their noses up at anything green. What can you do? Julia Wolman explains

The most recent diet and nutrition survey carried out among 4- to 18-year-olds found that children are eating less than half the recommended amounts of fruit and vegetables in a typical day.

The research showed that 20 per cent eat no fruit at all in any given week and 60 per cent eat no leafy green vegetables (an important source of iron and other essential micro-nutrients). It seems that these eating patterns are also influenced by social class, with those in the lowest income groups eating up to 50 per cent less fruit and vegetables than children in the highest income groups (1).

What are the benefits?

Children who get into good eating habits from a young age are likely to carry these through into their adult lives. They need to increase their fruit and vegetable consumption now to prevent serious diseases later on. Other good reasons for encouraging 'five a day' are:

■ Fruit and vegetables are full of fibre to help prevent constipation.

■ Snacking on fruit or vegetables can help to protect children's teeth and prevent excess weight gain by displacing sweets, biscuits and other sugary snacks.

■ Fruit and vegetables can make meals and snacks more interesting by adding colour, flavour and different textures.

What counts as a portion?

The good news is that there are so many different ways children can easily get their five a day. It's not just fresh varieties that count – frozen, dried, canned, juice, beans and pulses all count too. There are, however, a few rules.

■ Canned fruit should be in juice rather than syrup.

■ Low sugar, low salt canned vegetables (such as sweetcorn and chopped tomatoes) should be chosen wherever possible.

■ Fruit juice should be pure, preferably diluted for children and drunk only at mealtimes - a glass only counts as a portion once a day, however much is drunk.

■ Dried fruit is nutritious but has quite a high sugar content, therefore should only be eaten as part of a meal to protect children's teeth.

■ Beans (including baked beans) and pulses only count once a day – low salt/sugar varieties should be chosen

wherever possible. They count as protein foods as well as vegetables.

The best way to think about what consists of a portion for children is to use a child's handful as a guide. Therefore, depending on the age and size of the child, a portion may be: one small apple, two small satsumas, one tomato, a handful of peas or sweetcorn, and so on. The basic message for young children is to eat some type of fruit or vegetable five times a day.

Orange squash, blackcurrant juice drink, strawberry yoghurt, tomato ketchup and raspberry jam do not count, as there is not nearly enough fruit in them to make a portion. Potatoes fall into the category of starchy foods, rather than the fruits

Putting it into practice

Breakfast:	Handful of **raisins** on breakfast cereal with milk	(1 portion)
	Small glass of pure orange **juice**, diluted	(1 portion)
Lunch:	Jacket potato with cheese, **baked beans** and **salad**	(2 portions)
	Apple	(1 portion)
Dinner:	Spaghetti bolognaise (**frozen vegetables** added to sauce)	(1 portion)
	Tinned peaches with yoghurt	(1 portion)
Snacks:	**Carrot** or **cucumber** sticks with houmous dip	
	Smoothie – **fresh/tinned fruit**, **banana** and milk (or yoghurt)	
	Sandwich with cream cheese and **grated carrot**, or ham and	
	sliced **tomato** filling	(1 portion each)

and vegetables group, and do not count either.

The rainbow rule

Achieving five a day does not mean eating five apples or five bananas. Different fruits and vegetables all have different beneficial substances in varying amounts, therefore a variety should be eaten to get the best mix. For example, carrots, nectarines and mango are good sources of vitamin A, whereas red peppers, tomatoes and strawberries are good sources of vitamin C. Spinach and okra are good for calcium, and dried fruit such as raisins, dates and dried apricots contain iron and potassium.

The colours of fruits and vegetables give clues as to the vitamins, minerals and fibre that they contain. By offering the children in your care a 'rainbow' of fruits and vegetables over the course of a week, you can ensure that their bodies will be getting a good range of nutrients.

Putting it into practice

So, how does all this fit into the reality of a typical day? The suggestions here (see box on previous page) show how a healthy child can meet, and even exceed, the five-a-day target. (Please note: this example is meant only as a guide).

What's the alternative?

Most child carers will at some point have experiences with children who absolutely despise all fruits and vegetables and will not go anywhere near them, no matter how hard they are encouraged otherwise. Sometimes this is genuinely because they do not like the taste or texture, but other times it is simply down to fear of the unknown. Whatever the reason, poor fruit and vegetable consumption can be a huge worry to parents and carers, who may opt for one of the many child-friendly supplements available on the shelves.

Vitamin and mineral supplements can be a useful safeguard against nutritional deficiencies for some children. Fussy eaters and those with a poor appetite may benefit from a supplement of vitamins A, C and D, and possibly iron too, but advice should be sought from the child's GP, health visitor or school nurse first.

However, supplements are not recommended as an easy alternative to the real thing. Health experts increasingly suggest that it is the combinations of nutrients, fibre and other beneficial substances that occur naturally in fruits and vegetables which bring about their protective properties. These combinations are not usually found in artificially produced supplements, so it is best not to rely on them completely.

References

(1) *National Diet and Nutrition Survey: Young People Aged 4-18 Years* Gregory *et al* (The Stationery Office 2000)

(2) 'Modifying children's food preferences: the effects of exposure and reward on acceptance of an unfamiliar vegetable' Wardle *et al* (*European Journal of Clinical Nutrition* 57(2): 341-8 2003)

Julia Wolman, registered public health nutritionist.

Encouraging children to drink water

Promoting the importance of drinking water gives pre-school children the chance to have a direct influence on their own health, says Alison Tonkin

Two thirds (66 per cent) of the body is made up of water, so it is easy to see why problems occur when water lost by the body, through breathing, sweating and going to the toilet, is not replaced. It only takes a 1 per cent reduction in body weight due to water loss to cause dehydration.

Even mild dehydration can lead to thirst, irritability and tiredness. As dehydration increases, the problems get worse and can include headaches, constipation and kidney and bladder infections. Encouraging children to drink small amounts of water regularly throughout the day helps to maintain health and general well-being.

Although young children are increasingly aware of what a healthy balanced diet is and the need to exercise, they are dependent upon the adults who look after them for the food they eat and the exercise they take. The promotion of drinking water provides children with an opportunity to have a direct influence on their own health.

How the body works

By explaining how the body works you can help children understand the thinking behind the good practices they are being encouraged to adopt. Children are surprised at how much of their body is made up of water and a practical demonstration of two thirds, say, of a circle, can be a good way to help them visualise it.

Making clear links with bodily functions will help children to appreciate the importance of drinking water. For example, we all lose fluid every time we go to the toilet. That fluid needs to be replaced.

Ask children to breath on a cold surface such as a mirror, and then look at

the moisture that has formed so that they can see that water is lost through breathing. Explaining why we feel hot and sticky after exercise is another good way to raise awareness of how water is lost. The body sweats to cool it down. This leads nicely into the need to increase water intake in warm weather or after exercise.

Making water available

Children do not instinctively drink fluids to replace those lost, so you need to supervise children's water intake. This provides a good chance to give simple explanations of how the body responds to different conditions and events and encourages children to respond to their body's needs.

The way you offer water can prompt children to practise different physical skills. Pouring water from a jug requires good hand-eye coordination, while a pump action dispenser needs firm pressure on a button or lever. Turning

a screw-top lid to open a flask or bottle provides yet another experience, as does filling the bottle in the first place. All offer good learning opportunities that allow differentiation between children's age and stage of development. As children grow in strength and confidence, so their ability to access water from a variety of sources will increase.

Giving children simple explanations about why drinking water can help them to stay healthy provides them with the information they need to make informed decisions and encourages positive health behaviour from an early age. By supporting them as active decision makers with regards to looking after their own bodies also serves to increase autonomy and self-esteem.

Alison Tonkin, lecturer and NVQ assessor in early years, Stanmore College, Middlesex.

National Standards
Criteria 8.1 of the National Standards for Under Eights Day Care and Childminding requires that fresh drinking water is available to children at all times.

For more information
HAPPY (Healthy Activities and Practices with Pre-school Years) is an early years health promotion initiative run by the London Borough of Barnet. It provides an integrated project approach to topics such as healthy eating, physical activity, dental health and accident prevention. For details contact: 020 8359 6343 liz.kelly@barnet.gov.uk

ERIC (Educational Resources for Improving Childhood Continence) ran the successful 'Water is Cool in School' campaign in 2002, which aimed to improve children's access to fresh drinking water in schools.

Telephone: 0117 960 3060 www.eric.org.uk

Water for me, please

By the time children feel thirsty, they are already dehydrated – which simply means the body does not have enough water to function at its best. Does your child drink enough water?

Dehydration can make children bad tempered and they are unlikely to know why they are feeling cross. By encouraging your child to drink small amounts of water regularly throughout the day, this can be avoided.

Although most children like drinking water and know that it is good for them, it is generally not their first choice because squash or fizzy drinks have a sugary taste that appeals more. If water is provided as an alternative to these drinks - which are a major cause of dental disease in young children - then gradually they will get used to it. Many pre-school groups, for example, offer only water or milk.

There are many ways in which you can encourage your child to drink water.

Turn it into a fun activity, such as a teddy bears' picnic. Fill the teapot with water and let your child practise their pouring skills.

Older children will enjoy the independence gained from helping themselves to water from a jug that has been put out for them to use. If they are encouraged to pour a drink for you at the same time, this also boosts their self-esteem and gives them great pleasure in doing something for you.

Alison Tonkin, lecturer and NVQ assessor in early years, Stanmore College, Middlesex.

Caution:
Once children begin to help themselves to drinks, it is really important to tell them that they can only drink from a jug or bottle if an adult has provided it for them.

Never put chemicals into a bottle that children associate with drinks. And remember to store all chemicals out of children's reach, preferably in locked cupboards.

What is dehydration?

Dehydration simply means that there is not enough water in the body.

Even mild dehydration can lead to thirst, irritability and tiredness, and as dehydration increases, the problems get worse. These can include headaches, constipation and kidney and bladder infections.

Encouraging children to drink small amounts of water regularly throughout the day helps to maintain health and general well-being.

Dental care for pre-school children

Dental disease can be prevented. Much of the disease occurs in children long before they come into contact with a dentist, so you are in a good position to help prevent dental disease because of your easy access to young children

Dental decay is still a serious problem in young children. Fifty per cent of five-year-olds in England have at least one missing, filled or decayed tooth.

Tooth decay often causes discomfort, unnecessary pain, infection and sleepless nights for both parents and children. If a child has dental decay it is likely that they will have unattractive teeth and may well be afraid to smile, and their self-confidence can be affected.

As a result of pain and infection thousands of children each year have teeth taken out under a general anaesthetic. This can impair both the speech and eating patterns of a child and often leaves them with a fear of dentists which remains throughout life.

No child should have to experience the problems associated with dental decay, a condition that is totally preventable.

Why do teeth decay?

Tooth decay is caused by the action of sugar and dental plaque (a sticky substance found naturally on the surface of teeth). The plaque and sugar react to form acid, which dissolves the surface of the tooth. Plaque is present in all mouths and is a soft, almost invisible layer of bacteria.

Toothbrushing: who's responsible?

Children don't have the manual dexterity that is needed to make sure teeth are thoroughly cleaned until they are about six or seven years old, but they should be encouraged to enjoy cleaning their teeth for themselves with help from a parent. Family fluoride toothpaste should always be used as this helps prevent dental decay and daily use can reduce decay by up to half.

It is brushing at home that is important. Brushing at nursery may not have an effect on what parents do at home. There can also be practical problems in large numbers of children brushing

Why good dental health matters in early life

Good teeth are important to help children eat and talk and feel confident.

Toothache is unpleasant. No parent would wish their child to suffer dental pain.

Habits established in early life are often continued through to adulthood.

their teeth in the day care setting; these can include supervision of brushing, staff training and the need for cross-infection control, caused by toothbrush sharing. However, where levels of tooth decay are high in under-fives, brushing programmes may be set up with the help of the community dental service.

Frequency of sugar

It's not the amount of sugar in sweet food and drink that matters, but how often there are sugary things in the mouth. This is why sweet drinks in a bottle and lollipops are so bad, as the teeth are bathed in sugar for a long time. Don't forget, sugar is turned to acid in the mouth.

If sugar is consumed at frequent intervals throughout the day the teeth are constantly under attack from acid. If this continues on a regular basis tooth decay will develop, which will eventually need attention from a dentist.

Knowledge of the process of decay can indicate the possible ways we can prevent dental disease.

One of the most important messages which you should try to give parents is to restrict sugary food and drinks as much as possible to mealtimes. Restricting the frequency of sugar intake rather than trying to eliminate sugar from the diet altogether is a more realistic aim.

Do pre-schools have a role to play in oral health?

The behaviours, habits and routines established in a child's early years are based on what they have learned from those with whom they spend a significant amount of time. Many children spend a lot of time with you, their pre-school carers.

- You have care of children during the period that dental disease first appears.

- You can inform and influence parents to make healthier food choices for their children.

- You can help establish healthy eating patterns.

Daily diet

The types of food and drink that children consume in early life can establish lifelong food choices. If a well-balanced, low sugar, diet is encouraged in the early stages of life it is likely that these acquired tastes will shape the future diet of the child.

Foods which contain high concentrations of sugar should be avoided between meals. Chocolate, sweets, biscuits, cakes and ice cream should be restricted to mealtimes only. Foods should be as varied as possible, and different shapes, colours and sizes should be used to make snack time fun as well as nutritionally sound. Healthy snacks include:

- Breadsticks, cream crackers, crisp bread or bread of any type.

- Dairy foods, cubes of cheese, plain yoghurt with chopped fresh fruit.

- Home-made plain popcorn.

- Sandwiches, rolls filled with meats (ham, beef, chicken), fish (tuna and salmon) or cheese.

- Peeled and chopped fruits and vegetables for example apples, tangerines, carrots, celery and tomatoes.

- Slices of pizza.

Drinks and nursing caries

Dental decay in front baby teeth, known as nursing caries, is a classic sign that a child has been drinking sugary drinks from a baby feeding bottle. When teeth are constantly bathed in a sugary liquid it causes the front teeth to decay rapidly and often turn brown in colour. Baby feeding bottles should not be used after the age of twelve months. The only drinks that should be served in a bottle are milk or water. Other drinks should be served in a feeder cup or an open beaker and kept to mealtimes only.

All drinks containing sugar cause tooth decay. Fizzy drinks and diet drinks can be acidic and if they are consumed frequently they can dissolve the enamel of children's teeth and so should be avoided wherever possible. So what should children drink and when?

- Milk is a nutritious snack-time drink.

- Water is the ideal choice for thirsty infants to drink throughout the day.

- Fruit juice (well diluted with water) is best served at meal times only.

- Sugar-free cordial, well diluted with water, can occasionally be used.

Going to the dentist

Children can be taken to the dentist as soon after birth as possible, even just to watch a parent or siblings have their teeth checked. A sympathetic dental team can get a child used to going to the dentist so that they accept treatment happily. Visiting the dentist on a regular basis will help the child see that it is not a place or experience to fear.

Dental treatment is free until a child is 18 years old. If you need information on where your local dentist is, you can contact the family health service authority, the community dental service or your health visitor.

Local dental care support

You may already be aware of the Community Dental Service (CDS) by another name, for example the school dentist or the dental clinic. The staff are trained to help communities improve their dental health, through education and by providing treatment and care directly.

Depending on local priorities and how high levels of tooth decay are in your area, the oral health promotion unit staff in the Community Dental Service can provide dental teaching aids and resources to enable you to give the correct help and advice to parents and their children. The staff from the oral health promotion unit may also be able to visit to talk to the staff, parents and children.

To find your nearest CDS, call your local NHS Trust and ask for the community dental service manager.

Kerry Davis, Oral Health Promotion Officer, Salford.

Getting weaning right

Weaning can be pleasurable, messy, frustrating and rewarding – sometimes all in the same day! However, getting weaning right provides firm foundations for good eating habits in life and so all the effort required is more than worthwhile, says Kate Harrod-Wild

In their first year, babies have to move from a liquid diet to an adult diet – learning to eat from a spoon, to chew, to feed themselves and drink from a cup. It is no surprise then that problems can emerge along the way. The weaning journey should be as uneventful as possible if you want to reduce the likelihood of feeding problems later on.

When to introduce solids

The Government recommends that six months exclusive breastfeeding gives most babies the best start in life. Where parents choose to bottle feed, they also suggest that this can be continued without introducing solids for up to six months. Families who choose to wean earlier should see four months (17 to 18 weeks) as the earliest time to start.

Weaning too early can lead to the baby having less nutrition overall. Research has found that babies who are weaned early can also be more at risk of allergies, wheezing and being overweight later in childhood. Weaning too late can lead to babies not receiving all the nutrition they need. There are also developmental windows for the introduction of tastes and textures, which the baby may miss if they are weaned too late.

Parents often believe that a baby is ready for weaning earlier than is appropriate. Questions they should ask include:

■ Does the baby just need more milk?

■ Is the baby going through a growth spurt?

■ Is the baby just awake and wanting to be entertained?

Up to six months – getting started

There are two stages of weaning up to six months:

■ Learning to eat from a spoon;

■ Acceptance of a variety of flavours.

If weaning starts nearer to six months, it is important to move through this stage quickly, so that the baby doesn't get behind – with development or nutrition.

Before weaning starts, plan ahead, getting the equipment you need (see box).

When starting solids, choose a time when the baby is happy and relaxed; make sure that they are not too full to try, but not so hungry that they will get frustrated with the spoon. Start with a puree made up to the thickness of single cream; baby rice is popular as a first food, but any smooth puree food is fine.

At the first attempt, the baby may struggle with one spoonful or eat several spoonfuls. Some babies may seem to spit out the food, as they may have difficulty moving it around their mouth at first. Keep trying once a day until the baby is used to the spoon, then start to introduce more flavours.

Begin with savoury flavours such as vegetable purees, which tend to be less well accepted; persevere over several days if a taste is rejected at first. Babies develop food preferences in their first year, so the more foods that are accepted at this stage, the less likely the baby is to be fussy as a toddler. To make sure that the solids are a good nutritional replacement for breast or formula milk, mix vegetable flavours with breast or formula milk, baby rice or a cheese sauce and fruit flavours with full fat yoghurt, fromage frais or custard.

Once the baby is taking five or six spoons at one meal, build up to two then three meals. As the amount of solid food increases, a baby's milk intake may start to decline. By this stage the baby should be having food from all food groups (see box below) to make sure that they are receiving a balanced diet.

Many toddlers have problems with iron deficiency anaemia, which can lead to poor appetite and development problems; this can be prevented by including good sources of iron in their diet every day such as meat, chicken, pulses (peas, beans, lentils, dahl) and fortified breakfast from about six months.

Home-made or bought foods?

Many people choose to use packet and commercial foods for convenience.

What you need for weaning

■ Baby spoons - flatter and softer than adult spoons

■ Small bowls - you don't need special baby bowls. Must be sterilisable

■ Spoon, fork and sieve - spoon and/or fork can be used to push food through sieve for home-made purees

■ Steriliser - for all equipment for weaning up to six months

■ Ice cube trays and freezer bags - freeze home-made purees into ice cube trays then push out into freezer bags for easy storage

■ Freezer proof pots - for larger quantities

■ Hand-held blender - not necessary but useful for making small quantities of puree

■ Bibs - bibs with arms or painting aprons can be useful once babies start feeding themselves

■ Flannel and/or wet wipes - for clearing up

■ Suitable seating - bouncy chair or car seat from four months; a highchair once baby is able to sit independently

■ Wipe-clean mat or newspapers - for under highchair

Some mistakenly believe that adult food is too rich for babies. However, they do taste different from 'real' food and it can then be difficult to make the transition, so try to mix and match with home-made foods.

Second stage (from seven months) jars tend to be purees with hard lumps such as vegetables in and many babies find these difficult to deal with. If baby foods are continued, choose a first stage (from four months) jar and mash with adult food (potato, rice, pasta, fruit, cooked vegetables and so on).

Six to nine months – learning to eat lumps and pieces

During this period, infants need to move on to:

■ Purees with soft lumps;

■ Finger foods.

This is when problems often start if carers either do not know they are supposed to introduce lumps and pieces, or stop trying because their baby refuses them or gags when offered them. If lumpy food is not introduced during this period, children are more likely to have feeding problems later.

Once babies start putting toys into their mouth (at about six months), they are ready to try finger foods. Start with foods such as banana, toast or a rice cake; gradually increase the amounts and types of foods (see box, below).

At the same time, start moving on to more textured foods. Add less liquid to purees and start foods that are more naturally lumpy, such as Weetabix and Ready Brek. Gradually start mashing some food instead of pureeing (potato, soft fruit, vegetables). As the baby becomes better at chewing, more foods, for example meat and fish, can be mashed.

Nine to twelve months – learning to eat with the family

By their first birthday, babies should be eating chopped food and feeding themselves with a spoon - at least part of the time. They should be joining in with adult meals and enjoying the social elements of food.

There is a common misconception that older babies and toddlers should be given 'children's food' such as fishfingers and baked beans. In fact, if introduced to a wide range of foods from an early age, babies and toddlers can and do enjoy foods such as curries, casseroles, stir fries and so on. Mild spices such as garlic, cumin, coriander and paprika can be introduced from the beginning of weaning, while hotter spices such as chilli and cayenne pepper can be slowly introduced from nine months.

Bottle to cup

A cup can be introduced from weaning and all drinks should be taken from a cup by the time the infant is 12 months old. Prolonged bottle feeding can lead

Finger food

First foods to try
Don't give any hard foods (raw carrot, raw apple) as the baby may choke. Remove any peel or pips. Fruit can be fresh, tinned or dried.

Banana, pear, kiwi, plum, peach, apricot, mango, toast, bread sticks, rice cakes, cooked pasta, cooked vegetables, cooked potato, chips, yam, plantain.

Later foods to try
Once the baby is managing the foods above (about nine months), the following foods can be tried:

Apple, harder pears, oranges, tangerines/satsumas, dried apricots, dried figs, dates, raw carrot, cucumber, strips of pepper, celery.

to several problems including over dependence on milk or juice, poor intake of solids and tooth decay. The cup should be of the type that allows fluid to come out if turned upside down. Valve type cups (non-spill) have been found to have all the same problems as bottles and are therefore not recommended.

Milk and water are the recommended drinks for babies; a thirsty baby will drink water. Fruit juices are popular as they are sweet and babies will drink them even if they are not thirsty. However, the acid and sugar in fruit juices are bad for babies' teeth and are not recommended.

Vitamin drops

All children should have vitamin drops after six months of age once they are no longer receiving 500ml (20oz) infant formula until they are five years of age. These can usually be bought (or are free to families on benefits) from health visitor clinics.

Kate Harrod-Wild, paediatric dietitian, Shropshire.

Food group	Examples	Recommended amounts by one year
Meat and alternatives	Lamb, beef, pork, chicken, turkey, eggs, peas, beans, lentils, iron fortified breakfast cereals eg Rice Krispies, cornflakes, Weetabix, Ready Brek	Give two to three times a day
Starchy food	Breakfast cereals, potatoes, rice, pasta, bread, naan, chapatti, yam, plantain, crackers, rice cakes	Give three to four times a day
Dairy foods	Breast milk, formula milk, cows' milk (on foods from six months, as main drink after one year), cheese, yoghurt, fromage frais	Give about three servings a day. One serving = cup of milk, small piece of cheese or a pot of yoghurt
Fruit and vegetables	Fresh, frozen, dried and tinned varieties	Give five tastes a day

From bottle to cup

How often do you see toddlers sucking from a bottle as they are being pushed around in their buggies? Government guidelines recommend that bottles should stop being used from the age of one. Julia Wolman explains why, and how you can help children make the move from bottle to cup

Cups should be introduced to children from six months of age and the aim should be for them to stop using the bottle from one year. It may seem easier to continue with the bottle, but it is very important that infants are given the chance to develop the new skills of sipping and swallowing instead of sucking. Babies can adapt quickly to changes around six months whereas it is harder for toddlers to develop these skills later.

Problems with long-term bottle use

Prolonged bottle use is associated with the following health problems:

■ **Tooth decay or bottle caries** – with a bottle, fluids are in contact with the teeth for long periods of time.

■ **Food refusal and fussy eating** – filling up on fluids by sucking endlessly from a bottle can reduce a child's appetite and interest in food. Also, sipping from a cup can help with learning to chew. With prolonged sucking from a bottle, it can be difficult to encourage chewing later and you may be left with a fussy eater on your hands.

■ **Nutrient deficiencies** – if fluids end up replacing food, a child may not get all the nutrients they need. In particular, iron deficiency anaemia may arise as milk is low in iron. Also if a child has not learned how to chew properly, they may not be able to chew meat, which is a rich source of iron.

■ **Poor growth** – iron deficiency anaemia may decrease appetite and prevent weight gain.

■ **Childhood obesity** – this may be likely if a child drinks a lot of high-calorie drinks from a bottle, as the sucking action makes it easy to consume too much fluid.

■ **Speech delay** – continual sucking from a bottle can mean that a child does not develop the proper tongue or muscle movements needed for good speech development.

Which cup?
It is easy to be confused by the huge range of children's drinking vessels available today. Some are non-spill and have a valve which controls the flow of fluid, requiring sucking similar to a bottle. These may appeal to parents and carers who are concerned about spillages. Other cups are free-flowing and encourage drinking by sipping and swallowing.

It is important that children are encouraged to develop this sipping skill, rather than sucking, which they have been doing naturally since birth. When choosing a cup:

Tips to encourage good cup use

■ Get children used to seeing the cup and let them play with it or use as a toy at first.

■ Let them see you using a cup – as their carer you are an important role model.

■ Hold the cup with babies and steady their chin to help them drink.

■ Encourage toddlers to use both hands to pick up and hold the cup – either hold it with them or be ready to catch it!

■ Use a small amount of water in a cup at first, no more than an inch – expect spills and try not to get annoyed. As with weaning, it's important to let children get messy as part of their learning and development processes.

■ Use praise and offer non-food rewards.

Look for those which
■ Are free-flowing

■ Encourage sipping

■ Do not have a valve

■ Do allow fluid to leak or spill when tipped upside down

■ Have two handles

Stay away from those which
■ Encourage sucking

■ Have a valve

■ Do not allow fluid to leak or spill when tipped upside down

Cups with removable lids or which are open-lidded are useful later, once drinking from a feeder cup has been established. Alternatively, give infants an open-lidded cup straightaway.

Which drinks?

Milk or water are the best drinks for babies and children, whether from a bottle or cup. (Under 12 months, cooled boiled water, expressed breast milk or formula milk are recommended). Most other popular children's drinks, such as squashes, other juice drinks, fizzy drinks and flavoured milks contain sugar or acid. These damage the teeth and also encourage a sweet tooth, often filling children up so they are not hungry for meals.

It is, however, okay to give children over six months a little pure fruit juice at the end of meals, as it can be a useful source of vitamin C, especially if the child is a fussy eater. Make sure that juice is well diluted – ideally one part juice to ten parts water – and offer only from a cup.

Consistent messages

Children should receive the same messages at home as they do when they are in your care. Make sure parents are aware of the disadvantages of prolonged bottle use. Explain that the longer their child uses a bottle the harder it will be for them to stop.

Tell parents about their child's achievements using a cup with you, and let them know what techniques you found helpful. Find out from parents if they have a suitable cup at home that they can carry on practising with. If they don't, find out which shops in the local area sell them so that you can tell parents exactly where to buy one.

You may meet some resistance from parents about using cups and getting rid of the bottle. They might say:

■ **'The cup spills everywhere when we are out'** – if using one of the recommended free-flowing cups then it is more likely that drinks will spill. However, some have fold-down spouts which would offer some protection against spills. If this does not reassure parents enough, then emphasise that it is their choice what to do when they are out, but they should at least try to use a free-flowing cup whenever they are at home.

■ **'My child won't settle at night without the bottle'** – this is a common situation which can cause frustration and anxiety for parents. Bottle use before bed, as a sleeping aid and during the night, can easily become a habit that is difficult to break. Babies and toddlers quickly learn to associate the bottle with security and comfort. It is important for parents to try to establish a bedtime routine that does not involve the bottle, and other non-food related ways of comforting their child during the night.

■ **'S/he doesn't like water'** – if you are faced with this scenario, encourage parents to gradually make their child's usual juice or other drink more and more diluted until they become used to a more watery taste.

If you feel a parent needs more support in helping their child move from a bottle to cup, always recommend that they speak to their health visitor for advice.

What else can you do?

If you work in a nursery or other early years setting, why not run your own awareness campaign with a bottle to cup week or monthly theme? Some organisations have a 'bottle bin' where parents are encouraged to dispose of their child's bottle and receive a cup or toothbrush kit in return. If budgets are limited, perhaps design your own leaflet or flier summarising the main messages about bottle and cup use and hand out to parents.

Learning to drink by sipping from a cup rather than sucking from the bottle (or breast) is a new skill for an infant or toddler. Moving successfully from bottle to cup will not happen overnight and may take weeks or months to perfect. Go slowly and at the child's own pace and, as with learning any new skill or behaviour, patience and persistence is key.

Julia Wolman, registered public health nutritionist, London.

Do you want to find out more?

Government guidelines: Weaning and the Weaning Diet (COMA HMSO 1994)

From Bottle to Cup Action Pack (Comic Company 2002) You may also like to visit www.comiccompany.co.uk and see their 'Cool Kids Use Cups' resources.

For more information about healthy eating and drinking for babies and children visit:

■ Food Standards Agency's website: www. eatwell.gov.uk

■ British Nutrition Foundation's website: www.nutrition.org.uk

Feeding toddlers and fussy eaters

The toddler years are when food can become a big issue. Kate Harrod-Wild, a paediatric dietitian, gives advice on how to help children eat well and establish good eating habits

Minor feeding problems are common in toddlers as they seek to assert their independence. However, if good eating habits are established during the first year of life, it can go a long way towards preventing these problems later (see *Practical Professional Child Care*, October 2004, 'Getting weaning right').

To provide all the nutrition a toddler needs, they should eat foods from each of the four main food groups every day (see box).

Drinks

Toddlers need about four to six cups of drink a day, more if it is hot or they have a temperature. The best drinks are milk and water, but only two to three cups of milk a day, as more can affect appetite. Fresh fruit juice can be offered at mealtimes. If you give children fresh fruit juice or squash between meals, dilute one in ten with water (some cups have a helpful line on to help you).

If a child is still using a bottle, move them gradually over to a cup to protect their teeth and discourage excessive drinking. Avoid valve type cups, which have all the same disadvantages as bottles.

Healthy snacks

Toddlers may need one to two snacks a day as well as meals, as they still have small stomachs and high requirements. However, snack times should be at least two hours before the next meal; discourage constant grazing as it can lead to poor appetite and overeating in different children. Many popular snacks such as crisps, biscuits, cakes and chocolate are high in fat, sugar and/or salt. Good snacks include any combination of the following:

- Fresh or dried fruit

- Vegetable sticks

- Toast, bread or crackers with Marmite or cheese spread

Food group	Which foods?	How often?	What do they provide?
Meat and alternatives	Lamb, beef, pork, chicken, turkey, fish, eggs, pulses (peas, beans, lentils, dahl), nuts. Includes mince, cold meats, meat products	2 - 3 servings a day	Protein, iron and other minerals
Cereal foods	Breakfast cereals, bread products (including tea cakes, bagels, pitta bread, bread muffins, crumpets, malt bread), potatoes, rice, pasta, chapatti, plantain, yam	3 - 4 servings a day	Energy, fibre (if higher fibre alternatives), B vitamins
Milk and dairy products	Milk, yogurt, cheese, fromage frais, custard, cheese sauce	3 servings a day (one serving is a cup of milk, a pot of yogurt, a small piece of cheese or about 4 pots of fromage frais)	Protein, calcium
Fruit and vegetables	All fresh, frozen, tinned and dried fruit and vegetables	Five tastes a day. As a guide a 'taste' is equivalent to the amount a child can hold in their hand.	Vitamins A and C, fibre

- Fruit or savoury dips, for example pureed fruit, fruit yogurt, mashed avocado, tomato salsa, hummous

- Tea cake, scone or malt bread

- Fruit yogurt

Common problems

Constipation

This is common in young children. Offer enough drinks (see above for guidance). If a child will not drink enough, try high fluid foods such as jelly, custard, gravy and ice lollies made with fruit juice or fruit puree. Also increase the amount of fibre the child eats, for example high fibre breakfast cereals like Weetabix, puffed wheat or porridge, wholemeal bread, wholewheat pasta, all fruit and vegetables. If these simple measures do not correct the problem, parents should seek the advice of a doctor.

Iron deficiency: anaemia

This is the most common deficiency in young children. Symptoms include poor appetite, lethargy and irritability. A blood test at the doctor's will be necessary to diagnose the deficiency. If it is confirmed the child may be prescribed iron medicine to correct the problem; it is not well tolerated, but it is important that the toddler takes the medicine until the doctor confirms that they can stop.

To prevent iron deficiency anaemia, offer good sources of iron every day. These include:

Meat

Liver and kidney are the richest sources of iron. However, beef (including mince, beefburgers, sausages, corned beef and meatballs), lamb, pork and pate (not for children under one year) are also good sources.

Fish

Tuna, salmon, mackerel, sardines, pilchards and kippers are all sources of iron.

Bread and cereals

Iron fortified breakfast cereals, such as Weetabix, Rice Krispies and Shreddies, are a popular choice with children. Wholemeal bread, brown pasta and brown rice all provide more iron than the white varieties.

Dried fruits

Apricots, peaches and prunes are the best sources. Dates, raisins and currants also contain some iron. Try these as snacks instead of sweets.

Pulses/lentils

Baked beans, kidney beans, lentils and soya beans are good sources of iron. If you eat curries, try giving your child more dahl. Try lentil or bean soup.

Green vegetables

Spinach, broccoli, spring greens, kale, okra, watercress and rocket all contain some iron. Cooking vegetables for too long destroys their vitamin C content, so try steaming or stir frying instead.

Nuts and seeds

Most nuts and peanut butter contain iron. Cashew nuts, sesame seeds and tahini are particularly good sources. (Avoid nuts until three years if there is a family history of allergies.)

Miscellaneous

■ Egg yolk contains iron, but the iron is not easily used in the body.

■ Curry powder, quorn and tofu are good sources of iron for vegetarians.

■ Bombay mix, plain chocolate, liquorice and treacle all contain iron but should only be eaten in moderation, as they are high in fat and /or sugar.

■ As well as the extra iron, offer a source of vitamin C, such as fruit or vegetables, with every meal as this helps the iron to be absorbed.

Fussy feeders

Probably the most common cause of stress in parents and carers! Minor food refusal and fussiness is entirely normal at this stage. However, how it is managed can affect its duration and severity.

Ultimately, remember that a healthy child will not starve themselves – even if they have days when they eat almost nothing, they will not come to any harm; although it may not feel that way! Children grow in spurts, so they may well have weeks of having good appetites then weeks when they eat very little. If you are concerned that a child is not growing, or is losing weight, talk to their parents who should consult a doctor or health visitor.

Obesity

Unfortunately, this is an increasing problem, even among toddlers. If there are concerns about a child's weight they should have their Body

Tips for fussy eaters

- Offer very small portions so that the child has a realistic chance of finishing what is on their plate; they can always ask for more.

- Ignore food refusal and take the plate away without comment. Don't give endless alternatives, but do give foods that the child has accepted before; now is not the time to experiment.

- Praise any food eaten.

- Limit mealtimes to 20 to 30 minutes; you will both have had enough by then.

- If meals are not being eaten, do not allow to snack in between meals, as this will just reduce their appetite for the next meal as well.

- Watch drinking - it is tempting to offer a drink - particularly milk - to drink if food is refused, but this will just reduce their appetite for food.

- Do try to eat all together as much as possible - at a table without distractions such as the television. This will help to show that eating is a relaxed, pleasant activity.

- Don't force, coax or bribe the child to eat - this can put a child off eating altogether; or they may simply realise that not eating is a good way of getting attention!

- For older toddlers, a star chart can work well (in conjunction with reasonable portion sizes). Make sure rewards are not food related - they could be swimming, a trip to the park, colouring book, stickers - whatever the child sees as a treat.

- Offer fruit or salad only in between meals.

- Reduce the amount of snacks such as crisps, biscuits, sweets and chocolate offered. If you can, don't have them in the house as a temptation.

- Don't use food as a reward.

- Encourage a child to drink water rather than juice or milk between meals; if juice is used, gradually decrease the amount of juice in the cup over a period of time until the drink is nearly clear.

- Limit the amount of time the child spends watching television, playing computer games or otherwise sitting still.

- Take the child to the park, to play with a ball; walk rather than using a car, bus or buggy wherever possible.

- Don't make a big issue of the child's weight, but rather emphasise the benefits to everyone of eating healthily and being active.

Kate Harrod-Wild, paediatric dietitian.

Mass Index (BMI) – a way of comparing their weight for height – measured. Unlike in adults, a healthy BMI varies throughout childhood, so a chart is needed to determine whether they are overweight. If there are concerns about a child's weight, or to prevent weight becoming excessive in a child who comes from a family who are overweight (and is therefore known to be at higher risk), the following may help:

- Offer three meals a day. Avoid frying food as much as possible and increase vegetable portions. If they dislike vegetables make it clear that is the only extra food available.

Caring for vegetarian children

A child may be raised vegetarian for religious, ethical, health or environmental reasons, or simply the parent's personal taste preferences. With the correct information and planning a vegetarian diet can be perfectly balanced and healthy

Vegetarianism has different meanings for different people and the Vegetarian Society of the UK uses the following definitions:

1. Lacto-ovo-vegetarian – no meat or fish, but eats both dairy products and eggs. This is the most common type of vegetarian diet.

2. Lacto-vegetarian – no meat, fish or eggs, but eats dairy products.

3. Vegan – does not eat meat, fish, dairy products, eggs or any other animal product.

4. Fruitarian - a type of vegan diet where very few processed or cooked foods are eaten. The diet consists mainly of raw fruit, grains and nuts.

5. Macrobiotic – the diet progresses through ten levels gradually eliminating animal products and becoming increasingly restrictive leading to a diet of brown rice only.

The terms semi, demi or pesco - vegetarian may be used to describe the exclusion of all meat, but fish and other animal products are eaten.

Child health and development

There is no evidence to suggest that a well-thought out, balanced, vegetarian or vegan diet compromises child health, growth or development. However, it is generally agreed that children following the restrictive fruitarian and macrobiotic diets may be at risk of some nutritional deficiencies.

Health experts have documented several advantages of a vegetarian diet. For example, they are usually lower in fat, particularly the saturated kind, which can lead to lower cholesterol levels and a reduced risk for later development of heart disease. Vegetarian diets also usually contain more fruits, vegetables and pulses which increases fibre intake and

Important nutrients for a vegetarian child

Energy	Breads, cereals, potatoes and other starchy foods – in moderation. Add vegetable oils, vegetarian margarine, vegetarian cheese, milk, avocados or smooth nut butters to foods for extra energy.
Protein	Pulses (lentils, chick peas, beans), houmous, cereals, milk, cheese, eggs, soya products and tofu, nuts, seeds and meat alternatives such as Quorn.
Calcium	Dairy products, soya mince, dark green vegetables, bread, pulses, almonds, sesame seed paste (tahini*), houmous, tofu, fortified orange juice.
Iron	Dark green vegetables (spinach, broccoli, watercress), pulses, dried fruit (raisins, dried apricots, figs, prunes), fortified breakfast cereals, breads, tofu.
Vitamin B12	Dairy products, eggs, low-salt yeast extract, fortified breakfast cereals, vegetarian burgers and sausages.
Vitamin D	Dairy products, eggs, fortified margarines, fortified breakfast cereals.

* Sesame seeds may cause an allergic reaction in a small number of children.

contributes to good digestive health. Research shows that a diet with more fruits and vegetables can reduce the risk of heart disease, stroke and some cancers.

Variety is key

The first place to start in planning a healthy vegetarian diet is to make sure of a wide variety of foods daily to obtain the right balance of nutrients. The nutritional status of a child is only at risk if appropriate substitutions are not made for any group of foods that are omitted.

The four main food groups in a healthy diet are:

■ bread, cereals and other starchy foods;

■ fruit and vegetables;

■ meat, fish and alternatives (including eggs);

■ milk and dairy products.

For a vegetarian, either or both of the latter two food groups may need daily substitutions. The main nutrients provided by the foods in these two groups are shown above. Extra care is needed to ensure that a vegetarian child

obtains enough of these nutrients from meat-free sources.

Iron

Iron is less easily absorbed from plant food sources but consuming them together with vitamin-C rich foods or drinks helps to absorb the iron. Fresh or frozen vegetables, fruits and pure fruit juices all contain vitamin C. Iron absorption may be reduced by high-fibre cereals and bran-based varieties in particular should be avoided. Tea and coffee can also reduce iron absorption so should be avoided, especially at meals or within 1-2 hours before or after eating.

Fibre and bulky diets

Childhood is a time of rapid growth and development. Babies and children have high energy needs for their size but limited capacity to eat large amounts of food. Too many high-fibre foods can fill children up in small amounts. Instead they must eat small, frequent meals and snacks based on nutrient-dense foods that are not too bulky. For example, although wholemeal bread is generally recommended it may be best to vary it sometimes with white which is lower in fibre.

Milk

Full-fat milk must be given to children under two. Skimmed milk should not be given until five years. Soya milk is a good cow's milk alternative for vegans but brands must be fortified with calcium.

Vegan toddlers should use fortified soya infant formula milk as a main drink up until the age of two to ensure they have enough protein. However, soy-based infant formula milk contains a high amount of phytoestrogens which could affect the reproductive health of infants. Therefore it is recommended that soy-based formulas are only used for babies after receiving clinical advice. Any potential health risks are likely to be reduced after six months.

Processed meat – alternatives

Quorn and other processed vegetable protein products can be a useful addition to the diet of a vegetarian child. However, they can be quite low in energy and high in fibre. Some products can also be high in salt (sodium) so compare brands when out shopping and choose the one with the lowest amount. Always remember that variety is key and avoid increased reliance on processed vegetarian foods. Check ingredients labels for any nasty hydrogenated fats which may be listed as hydrogenated vegetable oil.

Nuts and seeds

Nuts and seeds are a good protein source for a vegetarian child. Whole or chopped nuts or seeds are not recommended for children under five because of the risk of choking. If either of a child's parents or siblings have any history of allergies such as hay fever, eczema or asthma, peanuts and peanut products are best avoided until after the age of three. All other nuts can be used either finely ground or as smooth nut butter spreads.

Supplements

A supplement of B12 may be needed especially for vegans and, if rice, oat or potato milk is consumed instead of cow's or fortified soya milk, a calcium supplement may also be required. An omega-3 fatty acid supplement may be useful for children who do not eat oily fish, such as salmon, sardines, mackerel or fresh tuna, but choose a brand specifically designed for children. Parents or carers should be encouraged to discuss their child's diet with a doctor before introducing supplements.

Vegetarian meal planning tips

- Remember to include a wide variety of foods daily and try not to use processed vegetarian products too often.

- If only one child in your care is a vegetarian, cook extra portions of vegetarian meals and freeze them to use individually another time.

- Encourage children to eat breakfast every day, preferably fortified breakfast cereals. Wholegrain is a good choice but avoid bran-based varieties.

- Provide two to three iron-rich foods every day alongside vitamin C-containing fruits, juice or vegetables.

- Add grated cheese or tinned (drained) pulses to dishes wherever possible.

- Encourage drinks of milk and water between meals and pure diluted juice with some meals. Avoid tea and coffee.

Julia Wolman, registered public health nutritionist.

Food intolerance: what you need to know

Food allergies and intolerance are more likely to emerge in infancy so if you provide full day care for babies and young children it could easily be you who spots the first signs. But do you know what to look for? And how do you care for a child who has a food intolerance?

Food intolerance is much higher in babies and small children than adults. Up to about ten per cent of all babies may be intolerant to a food. In babies with other allergic conditions such as atopic eczema, as many as one in three under the age of one may be affected. However, more than 90 per cent of children outgrow the intolerance by the time they are three. Quick onset symptoms – often the life threatening reactions – are less likely to be outgrown than the slower onset symptoms.

Intolerance or allergy?
Food intolerance refers to any reproducible adverse reaction to a food or ingredient, which is not psychologically based. (If someone retches every time they smell sour milk because they were forced to drink it as a child - this is a psychological response to a bad experience, not food intolerance.)

Food allergy is a form of food intolerance where there is evidence that the reaction is caused by the immune system's response to a food. This is a relatively rare form of food intolerance, but is more likely to cause life threatening symptoms.

How is it diagnosed?

Food allergy is easier to diagnose than food intolerance as the reactions tend to be more rapid. Evidence that the immune system is involved in the reaction is also more likely to be found by using conventional blood or skin prick tests.

The symptoms of food intolerance tend to take longer to appear, making the problem harder to diagnose.

Blood, skin, hair and other tests are available from alternative practitioners, in health food shops and by mail order, but there is little scientific evidence that they can diagnose food allergy or intolerance reliably. The only way to do this is to remove the food completely from the person's diet and see if

symptoms improve. If they get better and then worse again when the food is re-introduced, it is a good indication that they are intolerant to that food.

Many people see removing foods from the diet as a natural or low risk treatment. However, exclusion diets can cause nutritional and social problems, particularly for babies and children.

Suitable substitutes
Choosing a suitable substitute can be a problem, particularly for milk, where several options are available. The Government recommends that soya infant formulas should no longer be used as first line treatment for babies, because of concerns that they may cause long-term problems with reproductive health. Parents should, therefore, always consult a doctor who can prescribe a suitable alternative before changing their baby's milk.

For older children, there are alternatives to cow's milk made from soya, rice and oats, for example, but they do not contain the same amount of nutrition. Choose a calcium fortified milk wherever possible and seek advice from a dietitian on any vitamin and mineral supplements that may be needed.

Nutritional deficiencies
Problems that can occur include:

■ Poor growth.

■ Rickets – can cause problems with walking and bone deformities.

■ Iron deficiency anaemia – leading to poor appetite, low energy levels

Commom food allergens in the UK
■ Milk	■ Fish
■ Egg	■ Shellfish
■ Soya	■ Peanut
■ Wheat/gluten	■ Other Nuts

Symptoms of food intolerance
Quick onset	Slower onset
Asthma/breathing difficulties	Eczema
	Failure to thrive
Swelling of lips, tongue, mouth, throat	Colic
	Diarrhoea
Vomiting	Constipation
Rash	Reflux (vomiting and/or pain)
Anaphylaxis (collapse, unconsciousness, can stop breathing)	Migraine

and potentially problems with development.

Avoiding the excluded food
Sometimes it is believed that simply cutting down on a food may help, for example excluding milk, but still eating yoghurt or cheese. However, to give a child the best chance of growing out of their intolerance it is important that all traces of the food are removed from the diet. It is difficult to avoid a food completely as the term used for it on an ingredients list may be unfamiliar. Whey syrup, casein and lactalbumin, all contain milk, for example.

Social issues
Being on an exclusion diet isolates that person from their family and peer group and can cause tension, for instance:

■ Not being able to eat the same foods as everyone else.

■ Parental concerns about withholding foods, making mistakes, and so on.

■ Others not understanding the reason for/ importance of the diet and giving inappropriate foods/'treats'.

■ Other factors – lack of understanding of the diet, limited cooking skills.

All this makes it imperative that parents see a registered dietitian so that the family receive the support they need to make sure their child continues to grow and develop normally. Their family GP or a hospital doctor can make a referral to a dietitian. (For further information about dietitians, see the website of the British Dietetic Association at www.bda.uk.com)

Food challenges

Many problems such as atopic eczema, colic and diarrhoea can be caused by several factors and improvements following food exclusion may be coincidental.

Therefore, in most cases, foods should be retried on a regular basis. During a food challenge, the child is given increasing amounts of the excluded food – over hours or days depending on the foods and reactions involved. If the child reaches normal portion sizes of the food without a reaction, they can continue the food from that point. If they react, the challenge may be repeated in another six to twelve months. This is a step that is often missed. There are many older children – and even adults – on diets that were started in infancy because food challenge has never taken place.

Food challenges should always be discussed with a doctor or dietitian to check that it is appropriate and carried out in a safe way; some challenges may need to take place in hospital, particularly if a child has asthma or has had a life threatening reaction in the past.

Caring for children with food intolerance

For most children, food intolerances give rise to symptoms that are uncomfortable rather than life threatening. However, the potential risk to life should never be underestimated and procedures need to be in place to minimise any of these risks, particularly where children have more than one carer. The following general principles apply:

- Clarify with the parents/carers:

  Foods involved

  How this was diagnosed

Symptoms produced

Treatment needed(inhaler, eczema cream, adrenaline pen)

Any special foods needed and which of those will be provided by the family

- Make sure all those caring for the child know about the child's intolerance and that there is a written care plan, including all the above, agreed with the parents.

- Keep records of what the child eats; if a child does seem to react to a food this will make it easier to identify the cause of the problem.

- It is important that all those who provide food for a child with a food intolerance know the importance of checking ingredients lists carefully and have full written information on which ingredients to avoid. Most dietitians are happy to discuss suitable menus/foods with childminders and nurseries.

- Ideally, high allergen foods such as egg, fish and milk should be tried at home first. If you give a child a new food, give only a very small amount and watch them for any evidence of a reaction afterwards.

- No child with a history of food intolerance or other allergic conditions such as eczema or asthma should be given peanuts or other nuts under the age of three.

- Try to minimise differences between the child on an exclusion diet and their peers, for example by choosing similar snacks to give to the other children, giving the child the same meal as everyone else, and so on.

- Be aware that a child may have their first reaction to a food in their childcare setting - with you - particularly if they have other allergic problems such as eczema.

- If a baby or child is having difficulty breathing, has reduced consciousness or swelling around the face, call an ambulance immediately.

Kate Harrod-Wild, paediatric dietitian, Shropshire.

Ingredients containing milk	
■ Whole milk	■ Yoghurt
■ Skimmed milk	■ Butter
■ Skimmed milk powder	■ Margarine
	■ Cheese
■ Casein	■ Cream
■ Caseinate	
■ Whey	■ Cottage cheese
	■ Lactalbumin
■ Whey syrup	■ Lactose
■ Milk solids	■ Sour cream

Understanding anaphylaxis

Childhood allergies are on the increase, and for some the symptoms can be severe and even life-threatening. David Reading provides some information about anaphylaxis and suggests ways in which staff and parents can work together to minimise risks

Peanut allergy receives a lot of media coverage but other foods and substances – such as sesame seeds, egg, milk and latex – are also the cause of alarming allergic reactions. What can be done to protect children who have developed an allergy?

The answer, fortunately, is that even the most severe allergies are manageable. Where parents and child carers are supported by high-quality medical guidance, and commit themselves to remaining vigilant when food is around, their child can remain protected from harm.

What is anaphylaxis?

The term we often hear for a severe allergic reaction is anaphylaxis – a condition in which the whole body is affected, usually within seconds or minutes of exposure to the offending food or substance.

Symptoms of anaphylaxis may include generalised flushing of the skin, a tingling in the mouth and hives anywhere on the body, all of which are not serious in themselves. But in some cases, symptoms progress rapidly to swelling in the throat, severe asthma and – in rare instances – collapse, unconsciousness and even death.

Deaths triggered by food allergy are virtually unheard of in children under the age of 13, but there is still very good reason to be prepared. The rarity of deaths in the lower age group may be explained by the fact that parents and other child carers can watch over allergic children, whereas the risks increase when children reach their teens.

In all cases, the defence against a serious allergic reaction is an injection of adrenaline (also called epinephrine) and this must be administered as soon as a severe reaction is suspected. For this reason, an adrenaline 'pen' is prescribed to those suspected to be at risk, and this should always be readily to hand, whether the child is at home, visiting grandparents, at pre-school or school, or anywhere else for that matter.

Any allergic reaction, including anaphylaxis, occurs because the body's immune system over-reacts in response to the presence of a foreign substance, which it wrongly perceives as a threat. There is a sudden release of chemical substances, including histamine, from cells in the blood and tissues where they are stored. The release is triggered by the reaction between the allergic sort of antibodies (IgE) with the substance (allergen) causing the anaphylactic reaction. This mechanism is so sensitive that unbelievably small quantities of the allergen can cause a reaction. The released chemicals act on blood vessels to cause the swelling and low blood pressure, and on the lungs to cause asthma.

Adrenaline (epinephrine) acts quickly to constrict blood vessels, relax smooth muscles in the lungs to improve breathing, stimulate the heartbeat and help to stop swelling. The adrenaline pens prescribed by doctors are remarkably easy to use.

What can you do to protect children in your care?

The first point to remember is that children with severe allergies are not sick in the normal sense and in most cases can enjoy the same activities and challenges as any other child. But, of course, special precautions need to be taken.

Symptoms include:

- itching or a strange metallic taste in the mouth
- swelling of the throat and tongue
- difficulty in breathing – due to severe asthma or throat swelling
- difficulty in swallowing
- hives anywhere on the body
- generalised flushing of the skin
- abdominal cramps and nausea
- sudden feeling of weakness (drop in blood pressure)
- collapse and unconsciousness

These symptoms usually occur within minutes of exposure to the allergen, although they can occasionally occur after a few hours. No child would necessarily experience all these symptoms.

Common causes:

- peanuts
- nuts
- sesame
- cow's milk
- eggs
- shellfish or fish
- insect stings
- natural latex (rubber)
- some drugs

'A child at risk of anaphylaxis presents a challenge to any pre-school group. However, with sound precautionary measures and support from the staff and the authorities, life in nursery may continue as normal for all concerned.'

It is important to draw up a management or health care plan together with the child's parents, remembering that the onus must be on the parents to keep you fully informed about their child's allergy. This management plan should include the child's name, address, date of birth and a brief account of the allergy as well as emergency contact details for a parent/carer and a second contact name and number.

A crisis may never occur, but it's important to remain prepared. Full consideration should be given in the plan to an emergency procedure. This should be drawn up with the help of a health professional, such as a family doctor, practice nurse or pediatrician, and kept with the records on the premises with a copy attached to the child's medication pack so it is readily accessible. All staff should be made familiar with this procedure, which would include assessment of symptoms, administration of medicine as appropriate, contact numbers and the ambulance procedure.

It is important that the parents explain what medication their child has been prescribed and what symptoms may occur, and there should be basic instruction from a health professional on when and how to use

the child's emergency medication. All staff will need to know where the medication is stored. This should be out of reach of children but readily accessible. It should be labelled clearly with the child's name and instructions for use.

Responsibility for ensuring the medication is 'in date' rests with the parent. Social services should be informed and your insurance company notified of the details. Make sure insurance arrangements provide full cover for staff acting within the scope of their employment.

Staff training

In the unlikely event of an emergency, the child will need prompt medical treatment and staff will need to know what to do. In many schools and nurseries, staff have volunteered to be trained to administer medication for the treatment of a severe allergic reaction. In the case of pre-school groups, training could be arranged through the health visitor, local school doctor or the child's consultant. The community child health clinic may offer advice. Videos produced by the Anaphylaxis Campaign are useful resources to have at hand to show any new staff or parent helpers and could be included on a staff/ committee meeting agenda as a means of raising awareness.

Precautionary measures

Care should obviously be taken when preparing food and vigilance should be ongoing, with a commitment to reading food labels scrupulously. The parents can be called on for advice. If a child is, for example, allergic to peanuts, it would be prudent to exclude all peanut products from the premises.

Staff should also be aware of the possible risks posed by pet food which contains seeds and nuts and items used in science or nature activities as well as nut cereal packets for junk modelling.

A child at risk of anaphylaxis presents a challenge to any pre-school group. However, with sound precautionary measures and support from the staff and the authorities, life in nursery may continue as normal for all concerned.

David Reading, Anaphylaxis Campaign.

If you would like further information, please send an SAE to the Anaphylaxis Campaign, PO Box 275, Farnborough, Hampshire, GU14 6SX. Tel: 01252 542029

Website: www.anaphylaxis.org.uk

Example of a health care plan

Child's details

Full name...

Address...

Date of birth..

Allergy..

Contact details

Name of parent..

Telephone number...

Second contact name and number...

Details of child's GP

Name ....

Telephone number...

Medication

Name(s) of medication...

Expiry details..

Storage..

Training

Names of staff volunteers..

Date of last training of staff...

Names of staff who are aware of procedures ....

Precautionary measures

1.

2.

3.

4.

Consent and agreement signed by parent

I agree to the staff taking responsibility

Name ....

Signature ....

Resources round-up

Leaflets

Department of Health Publications from: Department of Health PO Box 777 London SE1 6XH Tel: 0800 555777 They produce leaflets on Breast Feeding, Bottle Feeding, Weaning, Practical Food Hygiene and Nursery Milk Guide.

The Food Standards Agency produces most food-related leaflets from the Government, free of charge. Tel: 0845 606 0667 or visit their website www.food.gov.uk

Contact the British Heart Foundation for magazines and Artie Beat resources, including a magnetic and fruit and vegetable counter for children. The British Heart Foundation, 14 Fitzhardinge Street, London W1H 6DH Tel: 020 7935 0185.

The Irish Dairy Council publishes leaflets to be downloaded on healthy eating for a range of ages, educational resources appropriate for several key stages as well as updates and fact sheets which make useful background reading. http://www.ndc.ie/contact.html Tel: 00 353 1616 9726

The Dairy Council, 5-7 John Prince's Street, London W1G 0JN E-mail info@dairycouncil.org.uk Website: www.milk.co.uk

The World Cancer Research Fund (some free leaflets) publishes leaflets on healthy eating with wide age range appeal as well as fact sheets and reports. World Cancer Research Fund, 19 Harley St, London W1G 9QJ Tel: 020 7343 4200. www.wcrfhealthcheck.org

Reports and books

Food in Schools Kit. Deals with guidance for schools rather than pre-school. Available from the department of Health See above or www.foodinschools.org

The following are all available from The Caroline Walker Trust. *Eating Well for Under-Fives in Childcare.* (£20.00) Practical and nutritional guidelines (second edition). This report by an expert working group gives practical advice on food choice and presentation of food to encourage healthy eating among pre-school children. It has an extensive resource list of its own and includes cookery books and books on learning through play.

Eating Well for Under-Fives in Childcare – Training Manual (£20.00). Or if you purchase both £30.00 A simple training guide to the key findings of the report by the same name. Packed with clear information and practical tips about good nutrition, it helps those who care for under fives put the theory of healthy eating into practice. It also includes a CD Rom which contains a database of foods drinks and recipes for the under 5's in childcare.

NMP U5 – nutrition analysis software, from the team who produced the Chomp Menu Planner. NMP U5 incorporates the new edition of the "Eating Well for Under 5's in Child Care" (Second Edition July 2006)

The programme has the ability to look at different nutrients and costs when making menu substitutions. It also allows you to import data on ingredient costs, suppliers and pack sizes from third party procurement systems and to export data on nutritional analysis and costs to Excel ™. For more information and costs visit www.nutmeg-uk.com or The Caroline Walker Trust, 22 Kindersley Way, Abbots Langley, Hertfordshire WD5 0DQ Tel: 01923 269902 Fax: 01923 445374 Also see websites (below).

From Kid to Super Kid by Paul Sacher. 'From Kid to Super kid' is not a diet book for children; the author, who is a state-registered dietician, is quite clear that children's diets should not be restricted nor should they be forced to lose weight. This could cause the child to miss out on all the nutrients which a growing child need to get from their diet. Instead it shows how to change your children's diet to a healthier one and how to help your child become more active.

Health events

Look out for national and local health promotion campaigns. Your local Health Promotion Department will have up to date details of national events and also information on any local initiatives and events. Additional resources are sometimes produced to support these. Examples are:

National School Meals Week.

This annual event seeks to create a positive link between the classroom and the service area. It is organized by the Local authority Caterers Association (LACA). It is usually in mid September. For more information visit www. teachernet. gov.uk (Also LACA website www. laca.co.uk

National Breakfast Week

■ Local health promotion departments will often provide a list of other campaigns with dates

■ Weightwise – is the annual health promotion event of the British Dietetic Association. The target group for this event varies from year to year. Visit www.bda.uk.com for up to date information on this national event.

National Smile Month

Visit www.dentalhealth.org.uk National Smile Month is the biggest annual oral health campaign in the UK, delivering important oral health information to millions of people nationwide.

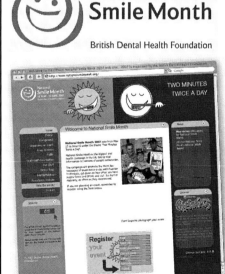

Websites

There are more and more good websites providing excellent information for teachers and others working with children. Also on the increase are interactive sites for children, although these are generally aimed at older children. I've included information on some of the best ones here.

You may well find links to other sites from here.

www.nutrition.org.uk
The British Nutrition Foundation

www.milk.co.uk
The Dairy Council website

www.welltown.gov.uk
For Key Stage 1 of PSHE. This is too advanced for pre-school children but may give you some useful information.

www.wiredforhealth.gov.uk
For teachers. Ideas for inclusion of healthy eating in the National Curriculum.

www.dh.gov.uk
Information about the scheme and promotion of fruit and vegetables.

www.bhf.org.uk
The British Heart Foundation website.

www.cwt.org.uk
You can view the whole range of materials produced by the Caroline Walker Trust here. It is also possible to have a demonstration of the CD-ROMs produced by the trust.

www.pre-school.org.uk
The website of a leading education charity contains pages under the title "Feeding Young Imaginations". Background and practical nutrition information is provided in a concise and clear format. It includes tips on implementing healthy eating in practice.